Girls, Gender and Physical Education

In this powerfully-argued and progressive study, Kimberly Oliver and David Kirk call for a radical reconstruction of the teaching of physical education for girls. Despite forty years of theorization and practical intervention, girls are still disengaging from physical education, dropping out of physical activity, with their health and well-being suffering negative consequences as a result. This book challenges the conventional narrative that girls are somehow to blame for this disengagement, and instead identifies important new ways of working with girls, developing a new pedagogical model for "girl-friendly" physical education.

The book locates our understanding of the experiences of girls in physical education in the broader context of young people's multi-faceted engagements with popular physical culture. Adopting an activist perspective, it outlines a programme of action informed by principled pragmatism and based on four critical elements: student-centred pedagogy, critical study of embodiment, inquiry-based physical education centred-in-action, and listening and responding to girls over time. It explores the implications of this new thinking for teaching, research, PETE and policy, and outlines a future agenda for work in this area.

Offering a profound theoretical critique of contemporary research and practice, and a new programme of action, *Girls, Gender and Physical Education* is essential reading for all researchers, advanced students and practitioners with an interest in the issues of gender, equity and inclusion in physical education.

Kimberly L. Oliver is a Professor of Physical Education Teacher Education in the Department of Kinesiology and Dance at New Mexico State University, USA, where she directs the Physical

Education Teacher Education Program. Working in the traditions of feminist, critical and activist research and pedagogies, her interest is in learning how teachers can assist girls in exploring, critiquing, and transforming the personal and cultural barriers that limit their health and physical activity opportunities. More recently, Oliver has moved into studying the impact that a field-based, student-centred and inquiry-oriented methods course has on pre-service teachers' abilities to be student-centred physical educators. She has published widely in physical education and general education journals.

David Kirk is Professor and Head of the School of Education at the University of Strathclyde, UK. He is an educational researcher with teaching and research interests in educational innovation, curriculum history, and physical education and sport pedagogy. Kirk is the founding editor of the peer-reviewed journal *Physical Education and Sport Pedagogy* (Routledge) and editor of the book series *Routledge Studies in Physical Education and Youth Sport*. He has previously held academic appointments at universities in the UK, Australia, Ireland and Belgium, and is currently Honorary Professor of Human Movement Studies at the University of Queensland, Australia. He has published widely on physical education and sport pedagogy and published *Physical Education Futures* (Routledge) in 2010.

Routledge Studies in Physical Education And Youth Sport

Series Editor: David Kirk, University of Strathclyde, UK

The *Routledge Studies in Physical Education and Youth Sport* series is a forum for the discussion of the latest and most important ideas and issues in physical education, sport, and active leisure for young people across school, club and recreational settings. The series presents the work of the best, well-established and emerging scholars from around the world, offering a truly international perspective on policy and practice. It aims to enhance our understanding of key challenges, to inform academic debate, and to have a high impact on both policy and practice, and is thus an essential resource for all serious students of physical education and youth sport.

Also available in this series

Children, Obesity and Exercise
A practical approach to prevention, treatment and management of childhood and adolescent obesity
Edited by Andrew P. Hills, Neil A. King and Nuala M. Byrne

Disability and Youth Sport
Edited by Hayley Fitzgerald

Rethinking Gender and Youth Sport
Edited by Ian Wellard

Pedagogy and Human Movement
Richard Tinning

Positive Youth Development Through Sport
Edited by Nicholas Holt

Young People's Voices in PE and Youth Sport
Edited by Mary O'Sullivan and Ann Macphail

Physical Literacy
Throughout the lifecourse
Edited by Margaret Whitehead

Physical Education Futures
David Kirk

Young People, Physical Activity and the Everyday
Living physical activity
Edited by Jan Wright and Doune Macdonald

Muslim Women and Sport
Edited by Tansin Benn, Gertrud Pfister and Haifaa Jawad

Inclusion and Exclusion Through Youth Sport
Edited by Symeon Dagkas and Kathleen Armour

Sport Education
International perspectives
Edited by Peter Hastie

Cooperative Learning in Physical Education
An international perspective
Edited by Ben Dyson and Ashley Casey

Equity and Difference in Physical Education, Youth Sport and Health
A narrative approach
Edited by Fiona Dowling, Hayley Fitzgerald and Anne Flintoff

Game Sense
Pedagogy for performance, participation and enjoyment
Richard Light

Ethics in Youth Sport
Policy and pedagogical applications
Stephen Harvey and Richard Light

Assessment in Physical Education
A sociocultural perspective
Peter Hay and Dawn Penney

Complexity Thinking in Physical Education
Reframing curriculum, pedagogy and research
Edited by Alan Ovens, Tim Hopper and Joy Butler

Pedagogies, Physical Culture, and Visual Methods
Edited by Laura Azzarito and David Kirk

Contemporary Developments in Games Teaching
Edited by Richard Light, John Quay, Stephen Harvey and Amanda Mooney

Sport, Fun and Enjoyment
An embodied approach
Ian Wellard

The Philosophy of Physical Education
A new perspective
Steven A. Stolz

Workplace Learning in Physical Education
Emerging teachers' stories from the staffroom and beyond
Tony Rossi, lisahunter, Erin Christensen, Doune Macdonald

Teaching Tactical Creativity in Sport
Research and practice
Daniel Memmert

Girls, Gender and Physical Education
An activist approach
Kimberley L. Oliver and David Kirk

Girls, Gender and Physical Education

An Activist Approach

Kimberly L. Oliver and
David Kirk

Routledge
Taylor & Francis Group
LONDON AND NEW YORK

First published 2015
by Routledge
2 Park Square, Milton Park, Abingdon, Oxon OX14 4RN

and by Routledge
711 Third Avenue, New York, NY 10017

Routledge is an imprint of the Taylor & Francis Group, an informa business

British Library Cataloguing-in-Publication Data
A catalogue record for this book is available from the British Library

Library of Congress Cataloging-in-Publication Data
Oliver, Kimberly L., 1967-
Girls, gender and physical education : an activist approach / Kimberly L. Oliver & David Kirk.
pages cm. -- (Routledge Studies in Physical Education and Youth Sport)
Includes bibliographical references and index.
ISBN 978-0-415-74926-8 (Hardback) -- ISBN 978-1-315-79623-9 (eBook) 1. Physical education for girls. 2. Physical education for girls--Social aspects. 3. Physical education and training--Study and teaching. 4. Gender. 5. Sports--Sex differences. I. Kirk, David, 1958- II. Title.
GV439.O55 2015
796.083'42--dc23
2015003737

ISBN: 978-0-415-74926-8 (hbk)
ISBN: 978-1-315-79623-9 (ebk)

Typeset in Sabon
by Fakenham Prepress Solutions, Fakenham, Norfolk NR21 8NN

MIX
Paper from responsible sources
FSC
www.fsc.org
FSC® C013604

Printed and bound by CPI Group (UK) Ltd, Croydon, CR0 4YY

For Kate and Annie

Contents

Preface

> If knowledge is constitutive of the world then our choices about what to teach, how to teach, and how to interpret the texts we teach are ethical choices. They are choices about the sort of world we want to live in. They are choices about what sort of life that world will support. They are choices about a consciousness that projects the world.
>
> Pagano, 1993, p. xv

We begin, each writing from our own perspective, on what brought us to this project. Coming from different countries, with different life experiences, in different phases of our careers, and with differences not only in gender but in how we see the world, including the world of academia, we merge our very different stances throughout this book. We conclude with what we both hope comes from our collective work to support creating better environments for girls to learn to value a physically active life; a world we hope our daughters and their daughters might have an opportunity to experience.

I (Kim) come to this project from a position of hope: a hope that all girls can one day find joy in and through physical activity; a hope that, as scholars, we might work collectively to bring about real change for real girls. I also come to this project inspired by some of the scholars whose words touched me in fundamental ways some twenty years ago and by others who have more recently inspired me. It has been through my inspiration that I have been willing to take great risks in my academic career; risks that I believe have allowed me grow as a scholar, as a teacher educator, as a woman, and as a person who works with adolescent young people.

I was sitting today, listening to a very wise woman, Linda, talk about trust. She said, "trust is a gift and yet we often think of trust as something to be earned". She went on to say, "when we trust in people we accept that at some point they will disappoint us". In that space and in that moment my inspiration for this project that David and I have been working on for eighteen months became crystal clear. For years I have seen how powerful an activist approach to working with girls in physical education is, if we can only find our ability to trust young people.

We will come to the idea of trust in Chapter 3, but it is here I want put forth the idea that "trust is a gift" and it's a gift we can each choose or not choose to give throughout our careers. For reasons that go so far beyond my understanding, it is a gift I have had the ability to give to adolescent girls across my entire career. In everything I have done with the participants I have been so privileged to work with over the years, the gift I have given of myself was the gift to trust that they had knowledge I so desperately needed. What I have learned is that in my willingness to trust in them I was given the gift of being able to listen and respond to their needs, their concerns, and to their interests, in ways that fundamentally changed me.

This ability to listen and respond to girls has not been an easy path by any stretch of the imagination because I learned very early on that to be able to listen to alternative perspectives takes a special kind of listening, and adolescent girls have brought many alternative perspectives to my world. Lisa Delpit (1995) talks about listening to alternative perspectives as she writes,

> To do so takes a very special kind of listening, listening that requires not only open eyes and ears, but open hearts and minds. We do no really see through our eyes or hear through our ears, but through our beliefs. To put our beliefs on hold is to cease to exist as ourselves for a moment—and that's not easy. It is painful as well, because it means turning yourself inside out, giving up your own sense of who you are, and being willing to see yourself in the unflattering light of another's angry gaze. It is not easy, but it is the only way to learn what it might feel like to be someone else and the only way to start the dialogue.
> pp. 46–47

Although these words and the words from so many girls have inspired me across the years, what is different now is that I have a greater understanding of the possibilities inspirational words can create. So in some sense, I'm coming to this collaborative project with the hope that we might inspire others in ways that I have been inspired by those who were brave enough to work on the margins, to work from places that others thought were impossible and unpractical, and who worked to create educational change for those we too often see as invisible. If even one line in our book inspires someone to want to work to make things better for girls, then I have done what I sought out to do. It is through genuine inspiration that the passion for change becomes possible.

I (David) have come to work with Kim on this book out of my concern over apparent lack of progress in this area of research in physical education over many years. I do not regard myself as a scholar of gender in physical education. Indeed, in the early years of my career it was a topic I actively sought to avoid, for reasons I will elaborate below. As I learned, it was impossible to do so and to fully engage with the issues and challenges that beset physical education as a field of practice. As my early studies of curriculum history revealed to me, physical education is a field socially constructed along the lines of gender division, even in countries where co-educational forms of organization have been in place for more than forty years.

In 1998 I returned to Loughborough University after fourteen years working in Australia and was immediately asked to lead a project for the Youth Sports Trust (YST), in association with Nike, called Girls in Sport (GiS). I wanted the project to be informed by the considerable amount of literature that was already published on girls in physical education and on gender issues more broadly, and along with the research team we put together an annotated bibliography and associated literature review that ran to many thousands of words. I was already familiar with Kim's early activist work with girls, and in 2000 invited her to come to England to provide some workshops for teachers and the research team on the activist approach she was already developing. Although the GiS project engaged with more than sixty teachers and thousands of young people, and produced a report I remain proud of (see Kirk et al., 2000), despite reasonable funding and a high public and professional profile, in my view it made very little difference to the disadvantaged situation of girls in physical education. It was hard for me to watch projects undertaken by the YST in association with Loughborough University in subsequent years that similarly failed to make any significant contribution and, compounding my concern, failed to even acknowledge or reference the GiS project.

Although I contributed a little to the gender and physical education literature following the GiS project, I did not become seriously involved in any similar scholarly work until 2011, when I received an invitation from UNESCO to write a 3000 word brief for fieldworkers and other practitioners in parts of Asia and Africa. This was a very challenging task, not least to keep the brief below 3000 words, but it also gave me an opportunity to reflect on and assess the progress that had been made since the early 2000s. I was disappointed to find that, apart from the line of activist research Kim has led and others such as Enright (Enright and O'Sullivan, 2012) and Fisette (Fisette and Walton, 2014) have contributed to, there seems to be little to celebrate in terms of the situation of girls in school physical education. The "same old story" of Chapter 2 reflects some of our thinking about the reasons for this lack of progress.

My active avoidance of researching gender in the mid- to late 1980s reflects, to some extent, the difficulty for men in physical education to become involved in scholarship that had until that time been led by women. Though lines of research on masculinities and boys began to emerge in the late 1980s (see, for example, Corrigan, 1988), it remained difficult for some years (for me, in any case) to come to position myself as a male physical education researcher in this field. It didn't help my confidence that my first ever, and only, data-based paper on boys, physical education and masculinity was rejected outright by *Sport, Education and Society* in the mid-1990s. Whatever the circumstances some thirty years ago, times have now changed. There is a thriving literature on boys and masculinities in physical education and sport as men have benefitted from the earlier work of feminist colleagues. But it seems to me that gender, despite its obvious importance and relevance, remains on the margins of the agendas of many physical education researchers.

Writing this book in collaboration with Kim is part of my (belated) recognition that gender must be of *central* concern to physical educationists. Moreover, I am convinced, given the lack of progress with the situation of girls in physical education for at least forty years and indeed the possibility of regression, that a particular kind of approach is essential, one that takes *direct* action to work pedagogically with girls (and boys) in physical activity and physical education settings.

In the quote that opens this Preface, Pagano makes clear that the choices we make about what and how we teach matter because they shape the kind of world we want to live in. The chapters that follow reflect choices we (Kim and David) have made, individually and together, about how we should approach working with girls in physical education. These are ethical choices at root because they aim to assist us as physical educators to make a difference for the better in young people's lives. As such, these are choices that matter for us; they describe what we think might be possible for girls as they come to value the physically active life.

References

Corrigan, P.D.R. (1988) The making of the boy: Meditations on what grammar school did with, to and for my body. *The Journal of Education* Vol. 170, No. 3, pp. 142–161.

Delpit, L. (1995). *Other people's children: Cultural conflict in the classroom*. New York, NY: New Press.

Enright, E. and O'Sullivan M. (2012). Physical education "In all sorts of corners": Student activists transgressing formal physical education curricular boundaries. *Research Quarterly for Exercise and Sport 83*, 255–267. DOI: 10.1080/02701367.2012.10599856

Fisette, J.L. and Walton, T.A. (2014). "If you really knew me" ... I am empowered through action. *Sport, Education and Society,* 131–152. DOI:10.1080/13573322.2011.643297

Kirk, D., Fitzgerald, H., Wang, J., Biddle, S. and Claxton, C. (2000) Towards "Girl-Friendly" Physical Education? A Report on a Large-Scale, School-Based Intervention. Invited paper presented to the International Congress on *Sport Science, Sports Medicine and Physical Education*, Brisbane, September.

Pagano, J.A. (1993). *Exiles and communities: Teaching in the patriarchal wilderness*. Albany, NY: SUNY.

Chapter 1

Introduction

An activist approach

> "The boys told me I couldn't play with them because I was a girl and I was Black... Some boys don't want the girls to play because they are girls and I think that's a real problem because we should all be able to do what we want to do. We should all be able to play." *Maggie Mae, age 10*
>
> "The boys also say that we are dumb, stupid and wouldn't last five seconds [in sports] ... and that you're a woman and you need to stay in your place." *Maggie Mae, age 10*
>
> "We can bring all the fifth-grade girls in and interview them and ask them how they feel when the boys say different things to them. I believe it will help, because it's not very fair for us girls and it doesn't feel very nice at all, because I know for myself that I do not appreciate it at all, and it's just a whole lot of chaos going around every day and you see different things happen to girls." *Maggie Mae, age 10*
>
> Oliver and Hamzeh, 2010, p. 43–44

We begin with the words of a 10-year-old African American girl who has articulated the "problem" as she sees it with girls playing, and has simultaneously outlined "what should be done" to address this problem. We have chosen to start here for two reasons: first, Maggie Mae shows us clearly how forms of race and gender inequity operate in her particular school to prevent girls from being physically active; second, and more important than merely showing the inequity, she shows us that identifying the problem is insufficient. We must do something, act in some way, to change this "problem" so that girls at this school can engage in physical activity without abuse from boys. In her 10-year-old fashion, she asked us as researchers to help her and other girls change their school so that all girls could play. *Herein lies the power of activist research.* When we work in collaboration and in action with participants we don't just, as Enright and O'Sullivan (2012) claim, produce different knowledge, we also *produce knowledge differently*. The difference is in the action: action directed towards challenging and changing barriers, identified by our participants, so that they might have better opportunities to play and to be active.

This book is intended to be a basis for action. In it, we seek to bring together, in one accessible volume, lines of research and scholarly advocacy in education and physical education stretching back to the 1980s, on work with girls, and with feminist and critical pedagogies. Although the book is intended to provide an accessible account of this research and advocacy, we see it not as any kind of definitive statement of an activist approach to physical education, but on the contrary, as a starting point for further research-based pedagogical action.

We start our introduction by briefly outlining the key aspects of activist research that have informed the body of physical education scholarship from which this book draws. First, activist scholars work from the belief that knowledge is produced in collaboration and in action. Second, they work from the belief that merely documenting "what is" is no longer sufficient with respect to understanding how to better engage girls in physical activity and physical education. As such, they move towards an intentional focus on studying "what might be" by collaborating with their participants to find spaces for change. Finally, activist scholars work from the belief that social transformation starts at the micro level in localized contexts. It is through this type of understanding that we can start to see where and how change is possible.

A first key aspect of activist research is that it is an "epistemology that assumes knowledge is rooted in social relations and most powerful when produced collaboratively through action" (Fine et al., 2001, p. 173). Activist scholars start from the belief that those with whom they work carry particular forms of knowledge, critique, and vision that is not obvious or automatically accessible to outsiders such as researchers (Fine et al., 2004). The activist researchers whose work informs the basis of this book have all worked from the position that girls themselves have insights into what does and does not work for them with respect to physical activity enjoyment and engagement. Activists work from the belief that valid knowledge is produced only in action: action with, not on or for, but action *with* participants. This is what sets activist work apart from traditional interventions that are designed and implemented by researchers without any collaboration with those who are the targets of such interventions (for example, McKenzie et al., 2004). This work is also set apart from those who do research "on" girls in order to "better understand" their perceptions (for example, Azzarito and Katzew, 2010; Azzarito and Solmon, 2009).

A second key aspect of activist research is the belief that merely documenting "what is" is no longer sufficient with respect to understanding how to better engage girls in physical activity and physical education. Much of the activist research in physical education draws heavily on feminist and critical pedagogies with a strong commitment towards social justice and social transformation (Fine, 1994; Freire, 1974; Giroux, 1997; hooks, 1995). Giroux (1997) writes:

> A critical pedagogy has to begin with a dialectical celebration of the languages of critique and possibility—an approach which finds its noblest expression in a discourse integrating critical analysis with social transformation ... [around] problems rooted in the concrete experiences of everyday life (p. 132).

Merging the language of critique and possibility, activists work from the perspective that understanding "what is", although necessary, is not sufficient and thus they are intentional in their collaboration with girls towards creating that "which might be". Part of moving from "what is" to "what might be" requires a shift in how we work with our participants. "By making girls' everyday experiences central to the research we are able to see the circulating discourses that shape their subjectivities, search for places to explore their agency, and work collaboratively with them to practice change" (Oliver, Hamzeh and McCaughtry, 2009 p. 93).

Finally, activists work from the belief that social transformation starts at the micro level in localized contexts. It is through this type of understanding that we can start to see where and how change is possible and as such we begin to write in ways that reflect what Weis and Fine (2004) note as critical to activist research:

> Our commitment to revealing sites for possibility derives not only from a theoretical desire to re-view "what is" and "what could be," but also from an ethical belief that critical researchers have an obligation not simply to dislodge the dominant discourse, but to help readers and audiences imagine where the spaces for resistance, agency, and possibility lie.
>
> Weis and Fine, 2004, p. xxi

Part of what the collective body of activist research in physical education illuminates is particular ways of working with girls that do seem to facilitate their interest, learning, enjoyment and engagement in physical education and physical activity. It is on this knowledge that our book focuses its attention.

The task for activist pedagogy: valuing the physically active life

Activists start at the local level. This is not only vitally important to the success of their work, but it is also possible to share an overarching goal for physical education with other activists working in other locales. This goal has to have a clear focus, it needs to reflect the unique contribution physical education makes in the school curriculum, and it needs to have the potential to make a difference for the better that everyone can embrace. This goal for physical education is for all young people to learn to value the physically active life. We believe this is the task for activist pedagogues in physical education.

Physical educators in many countries have a long history of commitment to the idea that the main purpose of school physical education is to facilitate the lifelong participation of young people in physical activity, typically in the form of sport, exercise or active leisure, dance, meditative and martial arts and outdoor adventure activities. Central to this purpose is the transfer of learning, from the school to life beyond the school, contemporaneously and into adulthood. This aspiration has often informed the standard "broad and balanced" programme of individual and team games, aquatics, gymnastics, dance, health-related exercise and adventure activities that is common to many countries across the world (Puhse and Gerber, 2005).

If we are to trust the many surveys of adult physical activity, it is an aspiration that physical education has rarely managed to achieve (Kirk, 2010). With some exceptions, for example, in the Scandinavian countries, few adults who *do* engage in regular and lifelong physical activity do so despite, rather than because of, their school physical education experiences (for example, Flintoff and Scraton, 2001). Fewer still continue to participate in the games and sports that dominated their school programmes.

Despite our poor track record in realizing this common hope for physical education, we want to argue along with Siedentop (1996) that valuing the physically active life should be a main purpose of school physical education. If we could improve on the situation that currently exists, in small increments, this would be a truly *radical* aspiration that could provide significant benefits to individuals and society. Siedentop explains this notion of valuing the physically active life as follows:

> Valuing physical activity is most clearly revealed not in what we say or write about it, but in the decisions we make to arrange a daily or weekly schedule so that activity participation is possible even though there are other important or attractive alternatives. Although participation may be the key component in valuing physical activity, we must attend to a second component of valuing: willingness to participate in the sport, fitness, and leisure activity cultures in ways that are literate and critical.
>
> By *literate,* I mean that persons are knowledgeable and activist cyclists, volleyball players, hikers, and the like. People should be knowledgeable about sport, fitness, and leisure, and be willing to use that knowledge as activist participants in helping to preserve, protect, and improve the practice of their activity.
>
> By *critical,* I mean that persons should understand the structural inequities in their local, regional, and national activity cultures that may limit access to activity based on irrelevant attributes such as race, gender, age, handicapping conditions, or socioeconomic status. Individuals should *value* fair access to participation so much that they are willing to work at local, regional, and national levels to make that activity more available to more people.
>
> Siedentop, 1996, p. 266

This definition focuses on *valuing*, a verb that implies something deeper, more committed and longer lasting that mere knowing or doing. Valuing the physically active life, according to Siedentop, is dispositional. Part of what it means to value the physically active life is to habitually and routinely make time to be active, even in the face of attractive alternatives, and his notions of literacy and criticality are also important. Literacy points up the fact that there are things to know *as part of* the act of valuing. Moreover, criticality suggests valuing is not an individualistic act, focused solely on the self, but recognizes social and physical cultural conditions, locally and more universally, and the need for a collective understanding of barriers and opportunities to be active.

As physical educators, we believe that a major aspiration for working with girls is that they develop a disposition to be physically active on a regular, sustained and sustainable basis. Without an experiential base in physical activity, we can have only a limited impact on girls' understanding of the barriers they face to valuing the physically active life. This physical activity must be purposeful and it must be meaningful to girls in the moments of their engagement or else learning to value the physically active life is less likely. The experience of purposeful physical activity also provides an essential basis for cultural critique, through which girls can learn to name, critique, negotiate and overcome barriers to their physical activity engagement or enjoyment. It is through this process that they can come to move beyond what *is* and to embrace what *might be*.

Pragmatism and the politics of possibility

In assisting girls to see what *might be* as a matter of concern in their everyday lives, activist scholars work within a politics of possibility that is at root a pragmatic process. Rorty (1999) has described humanity's pursuit of moral progress not as a mega, once-and-forever event, but "more like sewing together a very large, elaborate, polychrome quilt", which involves using "a thousand little stitches" (p. 86–87). Progress with aspects of social life such as morality does not happen all of a sudden. It takes place through many practices over time. We do not think it is appropriate for us as physical education pedagogues to wait until gender equity has been achieved before girls can fully engage in physical education and lead active lives. On the contrary, an activist approach seeks to take small steps to improve the life situations of specific groups of girls in local contexts in pursuit of the overarching goal of them learning to value the physically active life. We ask three pragmatic questions that form the basis of a politics of possibility: Can we make the situation for *these* girls better than it is currently? What would be better? *How* might we go about this task?

Our response to this first question is yes, but we need to qualify the answer. We think it is important to always be mindful that we do no harm. Furthermore, we have no magic one-size-fits-all solution that will work for all girls in all cases. Much depends on local circumstances and how global forces such as physical culture act upon these circumstances. Although there will be similarities between different locales, there will also be important differences. There will always be challenges in managing the tension between the local and the global, but our response to this question is nevertheless in the affirmative.

In our response to the second question, we think that a core task for pedagogues is to work towards the possibility that all young people might come to value the physically active life. This aspiration is radical not only because it has been hard to achieve so far, but also because of the significant benefits it could bring to so many people in terms of the quality of their lives. But precisely the form a physically active life takes will vary between locales and between individuals within each context. This variability creates a challenge for school physical education that has traditionally prescribed its subject matters as games, aquatics, gymnastics and so on, a challenge that is also faced, as Dewey (1938) noted, by student-centred pedagogy more broadly. This does not mean that "anything goes" in the name of physical education, a point we will return to later in this book. It does mean, though, that learning to value the physically active life is less likely when subject matter is uniformly imposed upon individuals. This is because a part of the process of *valuing* the physically active life is that the form this valuing takes has to be meaningful and feasible for each individual.

Here, Dewey's (1938) concept of experience is important as a basis for all learning. Dewey argued that experience is educationally valuable when it leads to further growth of an individual. Continuity on an experiential continuum involves the full-embodied engagement of an individual through interaction with others and with the environment, but as Dewey recognized, it also offers a significant challenge to teachers in ways that traditional content-centred education does not.

In responding to the third question, "*How* might we go about this task?", we understand there can be no simple "how to" list of teaching strategies or learning processes. Judgement is required on the part of teachers in how to work with girls in their specific circumstances. At the same time, as we suggest in the next section and throughout this book, we will offer some proposals based on previous activist research with girls that might be worth trying out. As we noted in the first section of this chapter, "how" we work within a politics of possibility rests on a belief that knowledge is produced in collaboration and in action (Freire, 1974; Fine, 1994). In this context, and further reflecting a pragmatic position, we think it is important to say that valuing the physically active life is a pragmatic aspiration *to work towards* rather than an endpoint to be reached. The notion of valuing the physically active life is a point of focus, a touchstone for our professional community. As circumstances change, our focus may well change. It is a priority now and, as far as we can foresee, in the short- to middle-term future. It is also a complex, many-sided process that might move us towards a tomorrow that is better than today for as many girls as possible.

Towards a pedagogical model for working with girls in physical education?

We have noted the importance of starting in the local setting for activist physical education and of working *with* girls to identify the barriers and challenges that they believe exist to their engagement with and enjoyment of physical activity. But there are at least two senses in which rooting our work in the local context does not limit us entirely to the local. One, as we have already noted, is the possibility of shared aspirations on a larger, more global scale, such as facilitating young people in learning to value the physically active life. Another is the transportability of ways of working with young people between locales, particularly ways of working that have produced promising possibilities.

In order to conceptualize this transportability of ways of working across sites, we are employing the notion of a pedagogical model for working with girls. This idea of a pedagogical model is developed elsewhere (Casey, 2014; Kirk, 2013). In its simplest form, it is a way of ensuring distinctive learning occurs through the tight alignment of learning with teaching strategies and curricula developed to suit specific contexts. In addition, pedagogical models have a distinctive major theme, critical elements that provide them with their unique form, and learning aspirations.

One of the valuable features claimed for pedagogical models is that they allow us to manage the tension between local and global contexts. It is possible to inform local work with insights that have been generated through other activist work. A common purpose of this work and the major theme of a prototype pedagogical model can be expressed here as "an activist approach to learning to value the physically active life". The line of activist research that has emerged over the past two decades has sought to assist youth in learning to value the physically active life by way of girls learning how to name, critique, negotiate and transform barriers to their physical activity engagement, enjoyment, and learning. We came to this type of idea by working with girls in student-centred, embodied and inquiry-based ways centred in action, and through listening, to respond to them over time. These latter four ways of working with girls form the critical elements of the prototype model. What this means is that the key theme, critical elements and learning aspirations emerged as a result of the analysis of the activist research that has been conducted and reported since the late 1990s.

However, we have inserted a question mark at the end of the heading to this section to signify that we are unsure of whether the development of a pedagogical model for working with girls *is* the best way to conceptualize this work. We share some of our concerns about this notion in the concluding chapter of this book. Nevertheless, we wish to put this idea up front in the introduction as we believe the challenge of balancing attention to local and global factors and forces is real and must be met. The proposal to develop a prototype pedagogical model, one that would need to be further tested in practice, particularly in order to "scale up" this work beyond the few activist scholars who have taken forward this line of research, is one we are not prepared to dismiss at this stage. We need to set out what we have learned from this line of research first, before re-considering in the concluding chapter the notion of a pedagogical model and of a research programme for future activist research with girls in physical education.

The chapters that follow can be viewed as a basis for a future research agenda in physical education that seeks to assist girls in particular, and perhaps young people more generally, to value the physically active life. Chapter 2 sets a context for our collaboration on writing this book; it explores the reproduction and recycling of what we characterize as "the same old story" about girls and physical education. Chapters 3–6 are offered as a means of breaking this reproductive cycle so that we might make a difference for the better in girls' lives. In these four chapters we focus on each critical feature of how activists have worked with girls in physical education. These features can be viewed as the critical elements that could give a prototype pedagogical model its distinctive shape. We stress here that *in practice* the four critical elements are woven together in activist research. As we have already noted, these critical elements have emerged from the work activists have carried out on the ground with girls and reported in peer-reviewed publications. They represent the common features of this work. We suggest these features or elements must therefore be present in any future work with girls that aim towards learning how to name, critique, negotiate and transform barriers to their physical activity engagement, enjoyment, and learning, in order that they will value a physically active life.

This book can be read as an agenda for future pedagogical research in physical education built on what we have learned from activist work with girls. Perhaps in future, if researchers feel it is warranted, in might also include work with boys. We offer this book in the spirit of Lawrence Stenhouse's (1975) notion that any pedagogical intervention should be thought of "not as an unqualified recommendation but rather as a provisional specification claiming no more than to be worth putting to the test of practice" (p. 142).

References

Azzarito, L.M. and Katzew, A. (2010). Performing identities in physical education: (En)gendering fluid selves. *Research Quarterly for Exercise and Sport, 81*, 25–37. DOI: 10.1080/02701367.2010.10599625

Azzarito, L,M. and Solmon, M.A. (2009). An investigation of students' embodied discourses in physical education: A gendered project. *Journal of Teaching in Physical Education, 28*, 173–191.

Casey, A. (2014). Models-based practice: Great white hope or white elephant? *Physical Education and Sport Pedagogy, 10*, 18–34. DOI: 10.1080/17408989.2012.72697

Dewey, J. (1938) *Education and experience.* New York, NY: Macmillan.

Enright, E. and O'Sullivan, M. (2012). Producing different knowledge and producing knowledge differently: Rethinking physical education research and practice through participatory visual methods. *Sport, Education and Society, 17*, 35–55. DOI: 10.1080/13573322.2011.607911

Fine, M. (1994). Distance and other stances: Negotiations of power inside feminist research. In A. Gitlin (Ed.), *Power and method: political activism and educational research* (pp. 13–35). New York: Routledge.

Fine, M., Roberts, R., Torre, M. and Upegui, D. (2001). Participatory action research behind bars. *The International Journal of Critical Psychology*, 2, 145–157.

Fine, M., Torre, M.E., Boudin, K., Bowen, I., Clark, J., Hylton, D., Martinez, M., Rivera, M., Roberts, R., Smart, P. and Upegui, D. (2004). Participatory action research: From within and beyond prison bars. In L. Weis and M. Fine, (Eds.), *Working Method: Research and Social Justice*, (pp. 95–120). New York, NY: Routledge.

Flintoff, A. and Scraton, S. (2001) "Stepping into active leisure? Young women's perceptions of active lifestyles and their experiences of school physical education", *Sport, Education and Society*, 6: 5–22.

Freire, P. (1974). *Pedagogy of the oppressed.* New York, NY: Seabury Press.

Giroux, H.A. (1997). *Pedagogy and the politics of hope: Theory, culture, and schooling.* Boulder, CO: Westview Press.

hooks, b. (1995). Killing rage: *Ending racism.* New York, NY: Henry Holt.

Kirk, D. (2010). *Physical education futures.* London, UK: Routledge.

Kirk, D. (2013). Educational value and models-based practice in physical education. *Educational Philosophy and Theory 45*, 973–986. DOI:10.1080/00131857.2013.785352

McKenzie, T.L., Sallis, J.F., Prochaska, J.J., Conway, T.L., Marshall, S.J. and Rosenguard, P. (2004). Evaluation of a two-year middle-school physical education intervention: M-SPAN. *Medicine & Science in Sports & Exercise, 36*(8), 1382–1388.

Oliver, K.L. and Hamzeh, M. (2010). "The boys won't let us play": 5th grade *Mestizas* publicly challenge physical activity discourse at school. *Research Quarterly for Exercise and Sport, 81*, 39–51. DOI: 10.1080/02701367.2010.10599626

Oliver, K.L., Hamzeh, M. and McCaughtry, N. (2009). "Girly girls *can* play games/*las niñas pueden jugar tambien*": Co-creating a curriculum of possibilities with 5th grade girls. *Journal of Teaching in Physical Education, 28*, 90–110.

Puhse, E. and Gerber, M. (eds) (2005) *International Comparison of Physical Education: concepts, problems, prospects*, Oxford: Meyer.

Rorty, R. (1999). *Philosophy and social hope.* London, UK: Penguin.

Siedentop, D. (1996). Valuing the physically active life: Contemporary and future directions. *Quest,* 48, 266–274. DOI: 10.1080/00336297.1996.10484196

Stenhouse, L. (1975). *An introduction to curriculum research and development.* London, UK: Heinemann.
Weis, L. and Fine, M. (2004). *Working method: Research and social justice*. New York, NY: Routledge.

Chapter 2

The same old story: the reproduction and recycling of a dominant narrative in research on physical education for girls

Introduction

Writing in the early 1990s, Patricia Vertinsky (1992) pinpoints the moment when things went wrong for girls and physical education: the implementation in various countries of equal opportunities legislation in the 1970s and early 1980s. This is not to say that all was well before this legislation was introduced, but its introduction created the issue that is the central topic to this chapter, a narrative about "the problem" of girls in physical education. The wider impact of this legislation was without question right and necessary. But where it touched on physical education, particularly in North America, the assumption was made that coeducational programmes would be more equitable than gender segregated programmes. This assumption was not warranted. According to Vertinsky, "equal access did not ensure equal participation" (p. 378). Instead, what the antisexist legislation did was put boys and girls together in physical education classes that were run according to boys' rules and standards. Even where legislation was framed in ways that allowed single sex programmes to continue, this watershed moment brought physical education for boys and girls into direct comparison so the seeds of "the same old story" were sown.

Vertinsky (1992, pp. 378–379) maps out the basic elements of the narrative of the same old story persuasively. What it came down to was that "if girls did not avail themselves of opportunities for play they were blamed for having the 'wrong' attitude". It was girls' fault that they did not like vigorous physical activity, that they did not want to compete to win, that they avoided physical contact, that they valued being with friends over being on the winning team, and that they dropped out of physical education in increasing numbers throughout their high school years. Much hope was placed on teachers to carry through this reform. But teachers who had taught and had been trained in single-sex environments, even those who were committed to co-educational physical education, struggled in practice to treat all students the same, as the equal opportunities rhetoric seemed to imply.

Much of the research Vertinsky (1992) cited in this paper already recognized the simplicity of the practices that seemed to flow from this well-intentioned legislation. On the basis of this work she was able to write:

> Efforts to promote participation tend to severely underestimate the ways that girls' perceived opportunities are already bounded by previous socialization into play and sport from early childhood, the level of support from parents, peers, and teachers (especially in the primary years), and economic opportunity, class, and race (p. 385).

Despite the efforts of generations of feminist researchers who have tried to shift the terms of the narrative from blaming girls to recognition of a complex interaction of factors centred on the patriarchal order, the same old narrative has resisted and persisted (Flintoff and Scraton, 2006).

Our purpose in this chapter is to show how the same old story about girls and physical education is maintained and reproduced by some researchers who study this topic, and by sections of the media who report on some of this research. We are concerned about the perpetuation of the same old story in the work of researchers and the reporters of this research because we think it is this group who should be leading the challenge to change this narrative. We believe we need to understand the extent of the contribution researchers of girls and physical education make to the same old story if we are to contribute to a process of bringing about change for the better for all girls.

We begin by summarizing the collective knowledge from social, pedagogical and historical research on girls and physical education overviewed by Flintoff and Scraton in their 2006 *The Handbook of Physical Education* chapter, before going on to examine some of the research literature post-2006 that we think produces the same old story in a variety of ways. Next we present a case study of the treatment of the report of a large-scale study in England by the media to show not only that newspapers and other media outlets are parasitic upon research but that they also invariably simplify, sensationalise and misrepresent the findings of studies of girls and physical education. In our conclusion we attempt to understand some of the trends in this research, some of the reasons it perpetuates the same old story, and what might be done to address this problem.

The same old story: what is the evidence?

Although most peer-reviewed publications on girls and physical education provide short reviews of previously published research, Flintoff and Scraton's (2006) chapter in the *The Handbook of Physical Education* is one of the few detailed reviews of research on this topic. The review is of course selective and has a particular focus. It also reflects the location of its authors, geographically and paradigmatically, with the chapter emphasizing English-language publications in Europe and the UK and including studies that are informed by feminist theory. Nevertheless, it is the only recent comprehensive published review of what we have learned from research about girls and physical education and thus provides us with a valuable resource to support our argument about the same old story.

Before they begin to review the pedagogical research on girls and physical education, Flintoff and Scraton remind us that there is a considerable historical literature on this topic. Women played a significant leadership role in the development of physical education in the UK and elsewhere since at least the end of the nineteenth century. The "female tradition", as Fletcher (1984) described it, was always controversial as girls' and women's participation in organized forms of physical activity challenged deep-seated social mores about femininity. These historical studies also remind us that the issues surrounding girls and physical education have existed in education systems for a long time. This point is important for our argument about the same old story because it has, over time, become deeply ingrained in the collective consciousness of populations, including the institutions that prepare physical education teachers. Although some things may have changed over this century in terms of girls and physical education, there have also been important continuities between past and present that are well established and very powerful.

Flintoff and Scraton note a general trend in the research on girls and physical education reflected in the pedagogy literature more broadly, which is a shift of the attention of researchers from concerns about teachers, teaching and teacher education, to curriculum and more recently to learners and learning. This is another significant outcome of their review, as the papers they cite in relation to girls' perceptions and experiences of physical education date with only one or two exceptions from 2000. In other words, we know more about teachers and the curriculum in relation to this topic than we do about girls themselves. Although we think there is some published work from the early to mid-1990s that Flintoff and Scraton did not include, we might pause to wonder why it has taken researchers so long to consider it important to listen to the voices of girls.

Their review of studies of teachers, teaching and teacher education and of curriculum provides some important insights. One of the most significant is that gender inequalities and stereotyping are part of teachers' own experiences. These are powerful normalizing processes that individuals can challenge only at personal risk and cost. Teachers are then among the primary agents for reproducing existing gender relations in physical education, not as individual choices they make but as part of wider, sedimented and powerful institutional processes. Flintoff and Scraton note research that suggests male and female teachers practice slightly different teaching styles, with women engaging with girls in more interpersonal ways, in contrast to male teachers' more direct instructional styles. Their review shows the vitally important role teachers play as models of gendered behaviour for girls and boys. It also shows how hard it is to change these behaviours, even when teachers themselves recognize that there is an issue and willingly engage in change processes.

The curriculum represents a further topic of study for researchers of girls and physical education. Fintoff and Scraton report that this research is strongly influenced by the historical legacy of separate sex classes and high levels of differentiation of activities deemed to be suitable for girls and for boys. This differentiation leads to strongly entrenched practices of "gender-appropriate" physical activities in the curriculum. They show that differentiation of activities has continued even when initiatives such as the National Curriculum Physical Education in England offered alternatives. At the same time, drawing on US research about the 1972 Title IX development, they show that legislation requiring girls and boys to be taught the same activities together in co-educational classes is not necessarily a step forward in equal opportunities for girls. They cite research that shows boys dominate co-ed classes, and that perspectives on the gender-appropriateness of activities remain in place.

Returning to the focus on girls, Flintoff and Scraton show that the research reports considerable variability of experiences and perceptions, suggesting there is no homogenous "girl" who shares the same experiences and perceptions as her peers. Some girls say they like physical education and some say they do not. Some girls like some activities and others different activities. Citing their own research reported in 2001, Flintoff and Scraton claimed that girls' participation in sport is problematically low, though again there was much variability in terms of intensity and extent of participation. Other research they cite showed that, for girls who *do* wish to participate in sport, compromises are often required in terms of the construction of their feminine and sexual identities. Flintoff and Scraton claim research also shows that others, including their teachers and their peers, perceive girls as being inferior to males in physical education and sport contexts. Citing work published in 2002 and 2003, Flintoff and Scraton claim that research had only just begun to consider the experiences and perceptions of girls from different ethnic, religious and social class backgrounds and how their opportunities to be physically active may be shaped by school, family and community. They propose the need for research on "difference and diversity" as a future focus of studies of girls, gender and physical education.

We suggest that this analysis of the research literature by Flintoff and Scraton provides us with a helpful means of supporting our argument about the same old story. It provides us with one source to consult, to determine whether and to what extent a researcher's claims of the originality of their research focus on girls and physical education is credible. This is particularly the case for research carried out after the publication of this chapter in 2006. But it is also the case for some research conducted before this in so far as Flintoff and Scraton provide us with a sense of the critical mass of studies that have investigated particular aspects of curriculum, teaching and learning.

Our own review of studies of girls and physical education since Flintoff and Scraton wrote their 2006 piece (sometime in 2004 or

2005) shows three distinct trends. The first is that researchers have indeed begun to answer the call to investigate issues of intersectionality, difference and diversity. The second is that some of the more recent research is located within the discourse of physical activity and public health, much of it utilizing public health research protocols centred on interventions. The third is that much of this research continues to perpetuate the same old story about girls and physical education.

A need to understand the intersectionality of the topic of girls and physical education, as we noted earlier, was identified by Vertinsky in her 1992 paper. Some researchers responded to this call. Oliver and Lalik (2000; 2001; 2004b) found that the intersections of race and gender were critical to how girls were learning to think about their bodies and recommended that teachers and researchers try to understand how this intersection influences girls' health-related choices. Benn and her colleagues (Benn, Dagkas and Jawad 2011) developed a line of research that has explored the experiences of Muslim girls in physical education in the UK and Greece. A paper by Azzarito and Solmon (2006) repeated the call for the exploration of intersectionality and difference, as did Flintoff and Scraton in their 2006 chapter. Azzarito and Solmon (2006) reported that young people's meanings of the gendered body intersected with the racial body and functioned to circumscribe girls' orientations towards and access to physical activities. They claimed that constructing more equitable physical education contexts and non-tolerance of sexism and racism should feature prominently in any physical education intervention.

Little of this work in physical education is cited or acknowledged in more recent studies of girls and intersectionality from a public health perspective. For instance, Grieser et al. (2006), as part of the Trial for Activity in Adolescent Girls (TAAG) programme, described an "exploratory study" that compared African American, Hispanic and Caucasian girls. What they found, in terms of the girls' attitudes, preferences and practices in relation to physical activity, was already in the literature. They concluded that other factors besides ethnicity impact on attitudes, preferences and practices towards physical activity. They also noted that girls may benefit most from interventions designed specifically for them, another point that was already well-established in the literature on girls and physical education. In a related publication reporting findings from the TAAG programme, Barr-Anderson et al. (2008)

noted that TAAG resulted in only modest improvements in girls' PA after three years and the improvement was only observed among girls who had been exposed to the intervention during their entire middle school experience.

In another study, Taylor et al. (2000) undertook an investigation of African American and Latina middle school girls on the premise that "more data are needed to better understand factors related to physical activity participation in adolescent girls" (p. 67). They concluded that "fun, social support, and concern with body image facilitated participation in activity. In contrast, negative experiences in physical education classes, concerns about appearance after activity, and lack of opportunity impeded participation in activity" (p. 67). They cite none of the literature reviewed by Flintoff and Scraton that had already established these factors, and report these findings as if they are new and original insights.

One of the earliest studies of physical education and physical activity levels from a public health perspective accidently stumbled across gender differences. McKenzie et al. (2004) reported the findings of the two-year long Middle School Physical Activity and Nutrition (M-SPAN) project that was among the first to promote the notion of Moderate to Vigorous Physical Activity (MVPA) as the "gold standard" outcome. They wrote: "A disappointing finding was that the physical activity increase for girls was not statistically significant ($P = 0.08$). This occurred despite the majority of PE classes being coeducational, permitting boys and girls to be exposed to the same teaching methods in the same classes" (p. 1386). As girls were not the focus of the study then it is perhaps not surprising that there is no research literature included on girls and physical education. Nevertheless, McKenzie and colleagues proposed that "this result suggests additional intervention strategies may be needed for girls, such as including activities more preferred by girls, single-sex activities, and different motivational and instructional techniques" (p. 1386). As Flintoff and Scraton's review showed, this proposal was already clearly established in the literature prior to the publication of this paper.

Further studies have adopted a public health perspective. An Australian study by Casey et al. (2013) of the Triple G (Girls Get Going) programme argued for the importance of recognizing that interventions developed in the USA, for example, may not work in other places such as Australia and that indigenous Australian programmes are required. A study by Felton et al.

(2005) reports on the Lifestyle Education for Activity programme (LEAP) in which girls were the focus, along with a concern for race and location (urban, suburban, rural). This paper reports a case study of one school's success in promoting physical activity for girls. Some researchers have continued post-2006 to study a range of topics relating to girls and physical education, invariably framed by concerns over low levels of physical activity and rising obesity, sometimes intersectional and sometimes not. These studies of factors influencing girls' participation in senior high school physical education courses (Gibbons, 2009), female students' perceptions of gender-role stereotypes (Constantinou, Manson and Silverman, 2009), and the effects of choice on the motivation of adolescent girls (Ward et al., 2008), contribute little in the way of new insights or knowledge.

These studies and others have in common either statements that appears to be "obvious" (for example, "Girls are more motivated when they have choices") or repeat information that is already in the public domain. Shen et al.'s (2012) ambitious study of urban African American girls' participation and future intentions towards physical education, which attempts to provide a gendered basis for the theory of planned behaviour by matching it to a feminist poststructuralist perspective, unaccountably fails to cite relevant and appropriate literature. Even well-conducted, theoretically sophisticated research such as Hills (2007) ethnographic study of 12- and 13-year-old British girls from a range of ethnicities and mostly lower socioeconomic communities repeats insights that have been in the literature for some time. That said, Hills brings together all three aspects of pedagogy – teachers, learners, and curriculum – to show that no one aspect provides an answer to the "problem of girls". When researchers such as Hills reveal this complexity, the response from other stakeholders, such as politicians, policy-makers and funding organizations, is typically to look for simple, ready-made solutions. A key agency in this process of simplification, and thus a key contributor to the perpetuation of the same old story, is the media.

Researchers and a parasitic media: a case in point

We argue the reproductive cycle of the same old narrative is maintained by research that appears to be neither regularly nor systematically informed by the collective body of previously produced and published knowledge of girls, gender and physical education. However, the research community does not accomplish this feat alone; it is considerably aided in maintaining the same old narrative by a parasitic media. To illustrate how the media comes in to play on the question of girls and physical education we will use a brief case study. The report we use is *Changing the Game for Girls*, published by the UK-based Women's Sport and Fitness Foundation (WSFF) in May 2012. The study was carried out in partnership with the high-profile UK-based organizations the Youth Sport Trust (YST) and the Institute for Youth Sport (IYS) at Loughborough University.

The following statement by the WSFF's Chief Executive provides an insight into how the WSFF position the report:

> This report presents new research that offers us the opportunity to begin to understand the causes of low levels of physical activity among girls. The project (the largest of its kind ever carried out in the UK) explores the views of girls – and boys – about physical activity, sport and PE, and the influence of schools, friends and families. It also includes interviews with parents and PE teachers. Importantly, the research points clearly to what can be done to help more girls get and stay active.
>
> Sue Tiball, CE, WSFF, 2012, p. 1

The claim is made that this is *new* research, and as such offers a *beginning* in the process of understanding girls' situations with respect to physical activity. It further claims it is distinctive due to its size and because it offers girls and boys an opportunity to be heard. Moreover, as Tiball writes, "importantly", the study provides insights into *how* to overcome the problems it identifies.

None of the claims made in the statement quoted are strictly accurate, and in some cases they seriously misrepresent much of the previous research that has been conducted. As we noted, Flintoff and Scraton's (2006) overview shows factors affecting girls' situations with respect to physical education and physical activity have been in the public domain increasingly since at least the mid- to late 1980s. Moreover, as their review shows, there have been at least as large-scale studies conducted previously, and a number of these studies that pre-date the WSFF 2012 report have also given girls and boys opportunities to be heard. Neither is its claim to focus on *how* to overcome the problem of girls' physical education original, notwithstanding the production of a "toolkit" for teachers, when set beside a whole line of other interventions, including activist research with girls. Finally, what the study claims to have discovered with respect to girls' and boys', parents' and teachers' views about physical activity, sport and physical education, including the influence of schools, friends and family, is not news. These insights have been in the research literature for at least two decades or more.

Perhaps the single most notable feature of this study is that it states in more explicit terms than is usually the case that school physical education as a curriculum topic, and teachers as agents, are very much to blame for many girls' unwillingness to participate. It is this point that was picked up in numerous media stories reporting the research on the day of the report's release. Jane Hughes (2012) for the British Broadcasting Corporation (BBC) website headlined her article with the statement "Schools urged to make PE more attractive to girls", while Emma Birchley (2012) for Sky News wrote "PE puts half of girls off exercise for life". Katherine Faulkner (2012) for the *Daily Mail* was somewhat more loquacious with her headline "Grubby changing rooms and embarrassment at getting sweaty in front of boys mean PE lessons are putting girls off exercise for life". *The Independent* journalist Richard Garner (2012), meanwhile, focused on a different finding, that "Unfeminine school sports leave girls on the sidelines", while his colleague, Harriet Walker (2012), with her commentary on these news stories, blamed "the psychotic gym teachers".

Although this "insight" may have been news to some of these journalists, calls for radical reform of physical education for girls have been appearing in the research literature for decades. As this report makes no claims to be an "academic publication", the lack of references is perhaps understandable. But Tiball's introduction, which completely omits to mention *any* other research on physical education and girls, rather than confirm the originality of this "new" research, merely feeds the reproductive cycle that lies at the root of the problem of bringing about genuine change that will benefit all girls to lead physically active lives.

Ironically, the IYS conducted another study that was covered in January 2005 by Denis Campbell of *The Guardian* newspaper under the headline "Ugly games kit turns girls off PE". Campbell (2005) writes of this earlier study:

> The findings of the survey, by the Institute of Youth Sport at Loughborough University, will be unveiled this week to the 250 delegates attending Let's Go Girls, the first conference in Britain on how to tackle young females' dislike of school games. The academics conducted research at 111 schools and among almost 11,000 girl pupils aged 11–16. They found that 30 per cent of the girls surveyed did not like their PE kit, and 40 per cent were self-conscious about their bodies. One in five said they only took part in PE because they had to, 15 per cent did not enjoy it and 3 per cent rarely took part. One in five believed that being good at sport was not important for girls and that it was not 'cool' to display sporting prowess. Worryingly, the researchers found that 30 per cent of girls did not think they would be physically active once they left school. They also discovered that girls become progressively more negative towards sport after the onset of puberty.
>
> www.guardian.co.uk/uk/2005/jan/16/health.schools

This passage could easily have come from the 2012 report or its associated media stories. Certainly it is difficult to see from this media report what progress has been made between the 2005 and the 2012 initiatives involving at least some of the same organizations. Although we, as researchers, might protest that our work has been misrepresented, we need to challenge this kind of media reporting of research-led initiatives surrounding girls and physical education and to undermine its simplifications and misrepresentations, while at the same time getting accurate messages across to the general public as well as key stakeholders.

Conclusion

We cited at length Patricia Vertinsky's 1992 paper to introduce the same old story about girls and physical education. We think it is significant that this paper is as contemporary now as it was then, more than twenty years ago. We think this says much about a lack of systematic research-led development in this field. At the same time, we concede that this deficit is characteristic of physical education more broadly. As we have tried to show in this chapter, some responsibility for the maintenance and reproduction of the same old narrative about girls and physical education must be borne by researchers and by the media reporting the findings of their research. We think there are a number of possible explanations for this situation, which suggest in turn potential solutions.

First, we think that this topic of study, like the broader field of physical education and sport pedagogy, is marred by poor citation practices and a consequent general lack of systematic building on previously published studies (Kirk, 2010). We might ask, has research on girls and physical education been too small-scale, or has it failed to be rigorous enough methodologically, so that this research isn't worth citing? But then, even if this was the case, why do successive studies, even those with standard public health designs featuring large numbers of participants, quantification and randomized trials, repeat the findings of previous research that has none of these features? Or perhaps the problem is that researchers from a range of fields, such as physical education and sport pedagogy on the one hand and public health on the other, are unaware of each other's work as they publish in different journals and attend different conferences? Although this may be an explanation for poor citation practices, it is not in our view an excuse, as any careful and thorough literature search should bring appropriate published research to light.

Second, poor citation practices may lie at the base of the apparently random, scattergun nature of research on girls and physical education. There appear to be few programmes of research and a marked absence of a broader programme of interlocking research studies that could produce genuine developments in practice. We need more evidence like we have from the activist research with girls that can illustrate what is possible in terms of improving the situation for girls and physical education. As researchers we could also develop a more assertive and collaborative relationship with media individuals and organizations so that the findings of research studies are reported accurately and that the "news" is highlighted and foregrounded in their reports.

Finally, we do not underestimate the scale of the challenge facing researchers to contribute to improving the situation for girls in physical education. We have suggested in the previous chapter that, as pedagogues, we must take a pragmatic approach, asking whether we can make a difference for the better, what "better" would be, and how do we go about this task? Instead of perpetuating the same old story, we could start with what we know about what *does* facilitate girls' interest, motivation, engagement and learning in physical education. Activist scholars could provide us with a lead to assist in answering the three pragmatist questions (for example, Enright and O'Sullivan, 2010; 2012; Fisette, 2011; Fisette and Walton, 2014; Oliver, Hamzeh and McCaughtry, 2009; Oliver and Lalik, 2004a; Oliver and Oesterreich, 2013). Through their change-focused research projects, they have identified some of the critical elements that *do* facilitate girls' engagement with physical education, including being student-centred, creating opportunities for girls to study issues of embodiment, inquiry-based education centred *in* action, and listening and responding to girls over time.

A large part of a shared mission for this field of inquiry is that it must become more focused on *how* we go about improving the situation for girls in physical education, building on what we already know from activist studies and other student-centred inventions. Learning from activist researchers, we explore in each of the next four chapters in turn these critical elements of programmes designed to work with girls in physical education.

References

Azzarito, L.M. and Solmon, M.A. (2006). A poststructural analysis of high school students' gendered and racialized bodily meanings. *Journal of Teaching in Physical Education, 25*, 75–98.

Barr-Anderson, D.J., Neumark-Sztainer, D., Lytle, L., Schmitz, K.H., Ward, D.S., Conway, T.L., Pratt, C., Baggett, C.D. and Pate, R.R. (2008). "But I like PE": Factors associated with enjoyment of physical education class in middle school girls. *Research Quarterly for Exercise and Sport, 79*, 18–27. DOI: 10.1080/02701367.2008.10599456

Benn, T., Dagkas, S. and Jawad, H. (2011). Embodied faith: Islam, religious freedom and educational practices in physical education. *Sport, Education and Society*, *16*(1), 17–34.

Birchley, E. (2012). PE "puts half of girls off exercise for life". *Sky News*. Retrieved from http://news.sky.com/story/14720/pe-puts-half-of-girls-off-exercise-for-life

Campbell, D. (2005, May 1). Ugly Games Kit Turns Girls Off PE. *The Guardian*. Retrieved from www.guardian.co.uk/uk/2005/jan/16/health.schools

Casey, M., Mooney, A., Eime, R., Harvey, J., Smyth, J., Telford, A. and Payne, W. (2013). Linking physical education with community sport and recreation: A program for adolescent girls. *Health Promotion Practice*, *14*, 721–731. DOI: doi:10.1177/1524839912464229

Constantinou, P., Manson, M. and Silverman, S. (2009). Female students' perceptions about gender role stereotypes and their influence on attitude toward physical education. *The Physical Educator*, *66*, 85–96.

Enright, E. and O'Sullivan, M. (2010). "Can I do it in my pyjamas?" Negotiating a physical education curriculum with teenage girls. *European Physical Education Review, 16*, 203–222. DOI: 10.1177/1356336X10382967

Enright, E. and O'Sullivan M. (2012). Physical education "In all sorts of corners": Student activists transgressing formal physical education curricular boundaries. *Research Quarterly for Exercise and Sport 83*, 255–267. DOI: 10.1080/02701367.2012.10599856

Faulkner, K. (2012, May 1). Grubby changing rooms and embarrassment at getting sweaty in front of boys mean PE lessons are putting girls off exercise for life. *Mail Online*. Retrieved from www.dailymail.co.uk/health/article-2138182/Grubby-changing-rooms-embarrassment-getting-sweaty-boys-mean-PE-lessons-putting-girls-exercise-life.html

Felton, G., Saunders, R.P., Ward, D.S., Dishman, R.K., Dowda, M. and Pate, R.R. (2005). Promoting physical activity in girls: A case study of one school's success. *Journal of School Health, 75*, 57–62. DOI: 10.1111/j.1746-1561.2005.tb00011.x

Fisette, J.L. (2011). Exploring how girls navigate their embodied identities in physical education. *Physical Education and Sport Pedagogy, 16*, 179–196. DOI: 10.1080/17408989.2010.535199

Fisette, J.L. and Walton, T.A. (2014). "Beautiful you": Creating contexts for students to become agents of social change. *Journal of Educational Research*, 0, 1–15. DOI: 10.1080/00220671.2013

Fletcher, S. (1984). *Women first: The female tradition in English physical education 1880–1980*. London, UK: Althone.

Flintoff, A. and Scraton, S. (2001) "Stepping into active leisure? Young women's perceptions of active lifestyles and their experiences of school physical education", *Sport, Education and Society*, 6: 5–22.

Flintoff, A. and S. Scraton. (2006). Girls and Physical Education. In D. Kirk, D. Macdonald, and M. O'Sullivan (Eds.), *The Handbook of Physical Education* (pp. 767–783). London, UK: Sage.

Garner, R. (2012, May 2). "Unfeminine" school sports leave girls on the sidelines. *The Independent*. Retrieved from www.independent.co.uk/news/education/education-news/unfeminine-school-sports-leave-girls-on-the-sidelines-7704402.html

Gibbons, S.L. (2009). Meaningful participation of girls in senior physical education courses. *Canadian Journal of Education, 32*, 222–244.

Grieser, M., Vu, M.B., Bedimo-Rung, A.L., Neumark-Sztainer, D., Moody, J., Rohm Young, D. and Moe, S.G. (2006). Physical activity attitudes, preferences, and practices in African American, Hispanic, and Caucasian Girls. *Health Education & Behavior, 33*, 40–51. DOI: 10.1177/1090198105282416

Hills, L. (2007). Friendship, physicality, and physical education: An exploration of the social and embodied dynamics of girls' physical

education experiences. *Sport, Education and Society 12*, 317–336. DOI: 10.1080/13573320701464275
Hughes, J. (2012, May 1). Girls and sport: Schools urged to make PE more attractive to girls. *BBC News*. Retrieved from www.bbc.co.uk/news/health-17873519
Kirk, D. (2010). *Porquê de investigar: Estado atual e tendências futuras nas pesquisas em educação física*. (Why research matters: Current status and future trends in physical education pedagogy.) *Movimento, 16*(2), 11–43.
McKenzie, T.L., Sallis, J.F., Prochaska, J.J., Conway, T.L., Marshall, S.J. and Rosenguard, P. (2004). Evaluation of a two-year middle-school physical education intervention: M-SPAN. *Medicine & Science in Sports & Exercise, 36*(8), 1382–1388.
Oliver, K.L., Hamzeh, M. and McCaughtry, N. (2009). "Girly girls *can* play games/*las niñas pueden jugar tambien*": Co-creating a curriculum of possibilities with 5th grade girls. *Journal of Teaching in Physical Education, 28*, 90–110.
Oliver, K.L. and Lalik, R. (2000). *Bodily knowledge: Learning about equity and justice with adolescent girls*. New York, NY: Peter Lang Publishing, Inc.
Oliver, K.L. and Lalik, R. (2001). The body as curriculum: Learning with adolescent girls. *The Journal of Curriculum Studies 33*, 303–333. DOI: 10.1080/00220270010006046
Oliver, K.L. and Lalik, R. (2004a). Critical inquiry on the body in girls' physical education classes: A critical poststructural analysis. *Journal of Teaching in Physical Education 23*, 162–195.
Oliver, K.L. and Lalik, R. (2004b). "The beauty walk, this ain't my topic": Learning about critical inquiry with adolescent girls. *The Journal of Curriculum Studies 36*, 555–586. DOI: 10.1080/0022027032000139397
Oliver, K.L. and Oesterreich, H.A. (2013). Student-centred inquiry as curriculum as a model for field-based teacher education. *Journal of Curriculum Studies, 45*, 394–417.
Shen, B., Rinehart-Lee, T., McCaughtry, N. and Li, X. (2012). Urban African-American girls' participation and future intentions toward physical education. *Sex Roles*, 67, 323–333. DOI: 10.1007/s11199-012-0179-6
Taylor, W.C., Yancey, A.K., Leslie, J., Murray, N.G., Cummings, S.S., Sharkey, S.A., Wert, C., James, J., Miles, O. and McCarthy, W.J. (2000). Physical activity among African American and Latino middle school girls: Consistent beliefs, expectations, and experiences across two sites. *Women & Health, 30*(2), 67–82. DOI: 10.1300/J013v30n02_05
Vertinsky, P.A. (1992). Reclaiming space, revisioning the body: The quest for gender-sensitive physical education. *Quest, 44*, 373–396. DOI: 10.1080/00336297.1992.10484063

Walker, H. (2012, Feb 11). I blame the psychotic gym teachers. *The Independent*. Retrieved from www.independent.co.uk/voices/commentators/harriet-walker-i-blame-the-psychotic-gym-teachers-7704401.html
Ward, J., Wilkinson, C., Graser, S. V. and Prusak, K.A. (2008). Effects of choice on student motivation and physical activity behavior in physical education. *Journal of Teaching in Physical Education*, 27, 385–398.
Women's Sport and Fitness Foundation. (2012). *Changing the game, for girls*. Retrieved from www.wsff.org.uk/system/1/assets/files/000/000/285/285/f4894dccf/original/Changing_The_Game_For_Girls_Final.pdf

Chapter 3

Student-Centred Pedagogy

"'Ask girls more about their opinion on what they want to do' and 'start listening to girls and hearing what they want to do and give them a chance at different things and encourage them more.' ... It's not that we don't like physical activity and sports; it's just that sometimes we don't like the kind of activities that people try to make us do, like basketball mostly, and sometimes we don't know what we like because we only get to try the same things all the time... If you want to get more girls active, you need to just listen to us and help us make our own clubs."

Enright and O'Sullivan, 2012a, p. 261

"In the final debriefing with the [youth] we asked them what they thought we did well. And one of them said 'we listened to their suggestions,' another student said that 'everyone participated.' And when we asked why we thought they all participated, she said 'it was because the games were fun, we got to make them, you change them to fit us and it was our choice.' So we can see how important letting them have a say in what they do really played into this." *Casey, Student Teacher*

Oliver and Oesterreich, 2013

Introduction

There now exists a strong and consistent body of research into physical education that demonstrates when teachers are student-centred in their pedagogical practices they can and do facilitate girls' active and willing engagement in physical education (Ennis, 1999; Enright and O'Sullivan, 2010a; 2010b; 2012a; 2012b; Fisette,

2011a 2011b; 2010; Fisette and Walton, 2014; Oliver, Hamzeh, and McCaughtry, 2009; Oliver and Hamzeh, 2010; Oliver and Lalik, 2004; Oliver, 2010). These findings support the repeated recommendations of scholars in physical education that teachers need to be student-centred if they are going to better facilitate young people's engagement (for example, Fitzgerald and Jobling, 2004; Glasby and Macdonald, 2004). The findings of these studies are also similar to other research on student-voice in the broader field of education (Cook-Sather 2009a, 2009b; Rogers, 2002; Rudduck and McIntyre, 2007; Schultz, 2003; Youens and Hall, 2006). This broader research has demonstrated that school reform and curricular efforts informed by student voice increases students' involvement, ownership and consequent learning (Beaudoin, 2005; Mitra, 2004; Cook-Sather, 2009a; 2009b; 2003; 2002; Wehmeyer and Sands, 1998).

In this chapter we begin by chronicling the research on student perspectives and student-voice in physical education research showing how the ideas around listening to young people emerged and how they evolved. In the second part of the chapter we discuss the research on student-centred pedagogy and how this differs from the physical education research on student perspectives and student voice. Here we highlight how activist scholars have utilized our collective understandings from the research on student voice, student perspectives and student-centred pedagogy in their work with girls as a way of better facilitating girls' active engagement in physical education and physical activity.

Research on student-centredness in physical education

Dyson's chapter in the *Handbook of Physical Education* is a useful point of reference for studies that lay claim to being "student-centred". He includes a wide range of studies under the heading of "student perspectives", including attitudes, motivation, voice, and perceptions. Dyson (2006) writes, "It was not until George Graham's monograph in the *Journal of Teaching in Physical Education* in 1995 that student voices emerged as a legitimate area of inquiry in mainstream physical education research" (p. 328). Graham's monograph was a landmark publication that brought to the forefront the need for researchers in physical education to understand students' perspectives. The authors who contributed to this monograph studied, for example, children's conceptions of ability (Lee et al., 1995), effort and skill (Veal and Compagnone, 1995), student alienation (Carlson, 1995), and learned helplessness (Walling and Martinek, 1995). In Graham's conclusion (1995), he advocates that we stop and listen attentively to the voices of students in physical education. This echoed similar calls from researchers in other educational fields at this same time (Corbett and Wilson, 1995; Rudduck and McIntyre, 2007).

Returning to Dyson's chapter we can see Graham's call was to some extent heeded. For example, some of the studies to which Dyson (2006) refers were located in urban school settings, concerned in particular with perspectives of young people from underserved communities (for example, Corbett and Wilson, 2002; Cothran and Ennis, 1999; Ennis et al., 1999). Other studies related to listening to student voice in curriculum development (for example, Brooker and Macdonald, 1999; Azzarito, Solmon and Harrison, 2006), related to students' experiences of physical education in general (Sanders and Graham, 1995; Portman, 1995; Suomi, Collier and Brown, 2003), or focused on student perceptions in relation to particular physical activities or pedagogical models (Tjeerdsma et al., 1996; Hastie, 1998; Kinchin and O'Sullivan, 2003; Pope and Grant, 1996; Hellison, 1996; Nilges, 2004).

Although Graham's monograph represents an important moment in the history of physical education pedagogy research, we should note that the authors in this collection cite literature that dates back as far as the 1970s and 1980s. There have been other "child-centred" moments in the history of school physical education, such as the educational gymnastics and modern educational dance movements from the 1940s to the 1960s. Educational gymnastics and related practices were child-centred in the sense that they focused on the individual rather than the group. However, as Fletcher (1984) showed, there was considerable continuity between the educational gymnasts and their Swedish gymnastics forebears in terms of teacher direction and control.

There has also been research that has had or has implied a student focus in physical education pedagogy. For example, elsewhere in the *Handbook of Physical Education*, Van der Mars (2006) summarized behaviourist research dating from the 1970s that utilized ALT-PE, centred on student behaviour, as a proxy measure of learning. This process-product line of research and its uni-directional path from teacher behaviour to student behaviour was challenged in the early 1980s by Walter Doyle's classroom ecology paradigm, which importantly, recognized the influence of student behaviour on teacher behaviour. Hastie and Siedentop (1999) noted, however, that as this line of research unfolded in physical education settings, most attention centred on the instructional and managerial task systems and almost entirely overlooked the student social task system.

Clearly, there has been an interest in physical education research and practice on the student dating at least from the 1950s. Graham's landmark monograph signalled an increasing focus in pedagogy research on student perspectives. From this research we gained insights into students' needs, motivation, and interests within physical education. Despite the innovativeness of the initial research on student perspectives, much of which focused on girls and their disengagements from physical education, we argue that this research has tended to be sporadic in nature and has set a pattern that has come to dominate research on students. As a result, we note that there is a lack of accumulation in this line of research, which, where it concerns girls, feeds the reproductive cycle of the same old story we noted in Chapter 2. Further, as we argued, these studies not only repeat the same findings over and over, but they also do not move our ability to better cater to girls' needs forward because they remain, in our view, at a relatively superficial level. These studies may be "student-centred" in so far as they take the student as their subject, but they fall short for a number of reasons, which we will show in the next section.

Four years after the publication of the *Handbook of Physical Education*, O'Sullivan and MacPhail (2010) published a book on young people's voices in physical education. In this edited collection they were careful to point out that the book was not merely research *on* students. They wrote, "we wish to avoid the notion that the authors who have contributed the chapters are interested only in 'consulting' young people ... Rather ... authors develop such consultation with a view to encourage young people's authentic involvement in opportunities for decision making, investment and participation" (p. 1). We believe that O'Sullivan and MacPhail (2010) are signalling a point that has repeatedly been made by activist researchers over the past fifteen years, that we must move beyond merely documenting young people's perspectives on physical education, physical activity and sport and start *acting on* what we are learning *with* youth to better meet their activity needs. In short, we must become genuinely student-centred not only in teaching but in research as well.

Student-centred pedagogy within an activist approach

To focus our discussion on student-centred pedagogy as a critical element to facilitate girls' active engagement in physical education, we draw on Cook-Sather's (2002) notion of authorizing student perspectives.

> To move more fully toward authorizing the perspectives of students is not simply to include them in existing conversations within existing power structures. Authorizing student perspectives means ensuring that there are legitimate and valued spaces within which students can speak, re-tuning our ears so that we can hear what they say, and redirecting our actions in response to what we hear. The twin challenges of authorizing student perspectives are: (a) changing the structures in our minds that have rendered us disinclined to elicit and attend to students' voices and (b) changing the structures in educational relationships and institutions that have supported and been supported by this disinclination (p. 4).

We believe that Cook-Sather's (2002) notion of *authorizing* student perspectives is important in our use of student-centred pedagogy for a number of reasons, all of which are ultimately about disrupting traditional student-teacher power relations and structures (Cook-Sather, 2002; Enright and O'Sullivan, 2010a; Fisette and Walton, 2014; Oliver and Hamzeh, 2010). In working towards a student-centred pedagogy, activist scholars in physical education have repeatedly disrupted traditional student-teacher power relations and structures, and as a result have gained important insights into *how* to better facilitate girls' engagement in physical education and participation in physical activity. This disruption of power has taken on particular closely linked characteristics including teachers' willingness and ability to learn to listen and respond to girls, an openness to change, genuine trust in girls having crucial insights into what better facilitates their physical activity participation, and an imagination for that *which might be*.

First, we show how student-centred pedagogy disrupts the traditional student-teacher power relations and structures that situate the teacher as all-knowing and the student as the passive recipient of knowledge (Freire, 1997). This disruption of power occurs when teachers value that girls have unique perspectives on their embodied worlds that teachers *do not have*. Given this valuing of girls' unique knowledge, teachers become actively willing to learn to listen and respond to girls with respect to what facilitates and hinders their active engagement in physical education. Teachers' willingness to listen and respond to girls disrupts the traditional educational power structures as Cook-Sather notes:

> Most power relationships have no place for listening and actively do not tolerate it because it is very inconvenient: to really listen means to have to respond. Listening does not always mean doing exactly what we are told, but it does mean being open to the possibility of revision, both of thought and action. At minimum, it means being willing to negotiate (2002, p. 8).

Activist scholars have consistently reported that when teachers *do* negotiate with girls with respect to creating curricula that girls believe better meet their physical activity needs, then girls take not only an interest in physical education, but also a level of ownership and responsibility. In this context, girls are willing to work *with* teachers to design curricula, assist in naming pedagogical practices that suit their physical activity needs, and work towards creating the type of class environment that better fosters their engagement. This disruption in traditional educational power structures that results as teachers actively listen and respond to girls, creates multiple shifts as Oldfather (2002) claims, "shifts on the part of teachers, students, and researchers in ways of thinking and feeling about the issues of knowledge, language, power, and self" (p. 87). At the same time, we recognize that different power structures require different forms of negotiation.

A second characteristic of how student-centred pedagogy disrupts the traditional student-teacher power relations and structures, that runs simultaneously with listening and responding, is teachers' openness to change (Cook-Sather, 2002; Enright and O'Sullivan 2010a; 2012a; Fisette and Walton, 2014; Oliver, Hamzeh and McCaughtry, 2009; Oliver and Hamzeh, 2010; Rudduck and McIntyre, 2007). Rudduck and McIntyre (2007) suggests that moving "from a familiar and safe position of power to a relationship that is more collaborative, open, responsive, and consultative" can lead to a "temporary destabilizing period of change for teachers" (p. 607). This point is echoed by Cook-Sather (2006) as she discusses that although change is a big idea, it is prerequisite for authentically engaging not only students' voices but also their embodied beings. Activist scholars in physical education have collectively been open and willing to change not only their thinking about *how* working with girls in physical education might look, sound, and feel, but have also been willing to change *how* they fundamentally think about and define physical education and physical activity for girls (Enright and O'Sullivan, 2012a; Oliver, Hamzeh and McCaughtry, 2009; Oliver and Oesterreich et al., 2015). As we elaborate more fully in the chapters that follow, when researchers and teachers "listen" and "respond" to the cacophony of girls' voices, we cannot continue to frame physical education in the ways we have done in the past, based on didactic teaching styles and sports-based curricula. Until we are open to seeing a different type of pedagogy of physical education, we will continue to hear the same old story about girls' (dis)engagement in physical education.

This activist research shows that adults start from where girls *are* rather than where adults think they should be and in so doing they assist girls in learning how to lead physically active lives in and out of school in ways that girls believe are relevant and appropriate for themselves (Oliver, Hamzeh and McCaughtry, 2009; Enright and O'Sullivan, 2010a; 2012a). An important insight of this research is that adults work *with* girls' femininities rather than *against* them. Consequently, what some girls view as appropriate engagement may be in direct contrast to conventional male-defined, physical activity participation (Thebege, 1985). Student-centredness does not assume there is only one way to be physically active, just as there is not only one type of girl; activist studies show how we can help all girls learn that they can find activities that suit their individual as well as collective needs and wants (Enright and O'Sullivan, 2012a; Fisette, 2012; Oliver, Hamzeh and McCaughtry, 2009; Oliver and Oesterreich, 2013).

A third characteristic of how student-centred pedagogy disrupts traditional student-teacher power relations and structures is trust. Activist scholars in physical education have started and continued their work with girls from the position of genuinely trusting that girls have crucial insights into what better facilitates their engagement in physical education. Cook-Sather (2002) highlights the importance trust has in educational policy and practice.

> Although it is rarely articulated as such, the most basic premise upon which different approaches to educational policy and practice rest is trust—whether or not adults trust young people to be good (or not), to have and use relevant knowledge (or not), to be responsible (or not). The educational institutions and practices that have prevailed in the United States both historically and currently reflect a basic lack of trust in students and have evolved to keep students under control and in their place as the largely passive recipients of what others determine is education (p. 4).

Chanan and Gilchrist (1974) are two of a plethora of child-centred educationalists writing in the late 1960s and early 1970s who showed how deeply institutionalized and normalized this lack of trust of young people is in school settings, a situation that Cook-Sather's work (2002) suggests has been exacerbated further over time. Thus we cannot underestimate how much of a challenge it is for teachers in today's schools to genuinely trust their students.

Trust is one aspect of activist research with girls that sets it apart from other research on student voice in physical education. Activist scholars display an openness to trust girls to be capable and willing to actively participate in a collaborative process designed to help facilitate their engagement in physical education and physical activity. They show a willingness to trust that the girls themselves might have a better embodied sense of what they need to feel comfortable in an activity setting and interested in learning to live a physically active life than we as adults. Additionally, they demonstrate willingness to trust girls by authorizing student perspectives within their pedagogies in ways that serve to benefit girls' educational experiences. Willingness to trust disrupts traditional student-teacher or adult-youth power relations as this means that teachers *and* researchers can no longer think that they have the answers. We must work from the position that in collaboration and action with girls we can figure out the answers to questions the girls themselves have posed while fully understanding that these answers will be context specific on the one hand, but on the other, the processes through which we come to understand might well have general similarities.

A fourth characteristic of how student-centred pedagogy disrupts traditional student-teacher power relations and structures that ties together willingness to listen and respond, openness to change, and trust that girls have unique knowledge, is an imagination for *that which might be* (Greene, 1995). Cook-Sather's (2002) notion of authorizing student perspectives quoted earlier acknowledges that we need to be willing to change "the structures in our minds that have rendered us disinclined to elicit and attend to students' voices" (p. 4). This becomes difficult if we cannot imagine something different, something possibly better. As Greene (1995) reminds us, "When people cannot name alternatives or imagine a better state of things, they are likely to remain anchored or submerged" (p. 52).

Imagination for that *which might be* thus becomes imperative if scholars are to move beyond how traditional physical education has shaped and limited the universe of possibilities for girls in physical education. This is what activist scholars have repeatedly done (Enright and O'Sullivan, 2010a; 2012a; Fisette, 2011a; Fisette and Walton, 2014; Oliver and Lalik, 2004; Oliver, 2010; Oliver, Hamzeh and McCaughtry, 2009). That is, they have created pedagogical possibilities in their work *with* girls that encourage the questioning of the status quo of physical education. They do not do this with the belief that they have the answers and that by facilitating girls' critique of the status quo they might reach some kind of Utopia. Rather, they come with the belief that by working together *with* girls they can co-construct alternative and better possibilities than girls currently experience. Activist scholars have learned some important insights into ways of supporting girls' physical activity participation from their intentional work *with* girls at assisting them in naming barriers and exploring, naming and enacting alternative possibilities that better meet their physical activity needs than traditional physical education (Oliver, Hamzeh and McCaughtry, 2009; Enright and O'Sullivan, 2010a; 2012b). The disruption of power relations and structures is thus about teachers continually challenging the status quo *with* girls as a means of seeking alternative possibilities that better facilitate girls' active engagement in physical education.

Conclusion

In this chapter we chronicled the research on student perspective and student voice in physical education noting insights from this work into young people's needs, interests and motivation. At the same time, we highlighted that there has been little systematic development of this research beyond a surface level or the repetition of what we already know. We argue that although physical education researchers have been documenting students perspectives, activist researchers were already working with girls and acting on what they were telling them in order to better meet the girls' needs and interests. Through this work what became clear is that traditional teacher-student power relations and structures were disrupted. This disruption came as activists were willing to learn to listen and respond to girls through negotiating physical education curricula, had changed their thinking about what physical education can be as a result of working with girls, had trusted that girls have crucial insights into what better facilitates their activity needs than adults, and created possibilities for girls to co-construct alternative and better physical education and physical activity possibilities.

Much of the research in physical education that has aspired to be "student-centred" has fallen short of this goal because it has equated student-centredness with merely listening to the voices of students. This has unintentionally fed the reproductive cycle of telling the same old story about girls' alleged problematic attitudes towards physical education. In contrast activists would argue we cannot be student-centred unless we create spaces for girls to inquire into what facilitates and hinders their interest, motivation and learning in physical education. As we show in the next chapter, centralizing girls' bodies pedagogically through inquiry-based approaches to learning is a crucial starting point for understanding girls' needs and interests.

References

Azzarito, L.M., Solmon, M.A. and Harrison, L. (2006). "...If I had a choice, I would..." A feminist post-structural perspective on girls in physical education. *Research Quarterly for Exercise and Sport, 77*, 222–239. DOI: 10.1080/02701367.2006.10599356

Beaudoin, N. (2005) *Elevating student voice: How to enhance participation, citizenship, and leadership*. Larchmont, NY: Eye On Education.

Brooker, R. and Macdonald, D. (1999). Did *we* hear *you*?: Issues of student voice in curriculum innovation. *Journal of Curriculum Studies, 31*, 83–97. DOI: 10.1080/002202799183313

Carlson. T.B. (1995). We hate gym: Student alienation from physical education. *Journal of Teaching in Physical Education* 14, 467–477.

Chanan, G. and Gilchrist, L. (1974). *What school is for*. London, UK: Methuen.

Cook-Sather, A. (2002). Authorizing students' perspectives: Toward trust, dialogue, and change in education. *Educational Researcher, 3*(4) 3–14. DOI: 3102/001389X031004003

Cook-Sather, A. (2006). *Education is Translation.* Philadelphia, PA: University of Pennsylvania Press.

Cook-Sather, A. (2009a). "I Am Not Afraid to Listen": Prospective teachers learning from students. *Theory Into Practice, 48*, 176–183. DOI: 10.1080/00405840902997261

Cook-Sather, A. (2009b). *Learning from student's perspectives: A sourcebook for effective teaching*. Boulder, CO: Paradigm.

Corbett, D. and Wilson, B. (1995). Make a difference with, not for students: A plea to researchers and reformers. *Educational Researcher, 24*(5), 12–17. DOI: 10.3102/0013189X024005012

Corbett, D. and Wilson, B. (2002). What urban students say about good teaching. *Educational Leadership, 60*(1), 18–22.

Cothran, D.J. and Ennis, C.D. (1999). Alone in a crowd: Meeting students' needs for relevance and connection in urban high school physical education. *Journal of Teaching in Physical Education, 18*, 234–247.

Dyson, B. (2006). Students' perspectives of physical education, in D. Kirk, D. Macdonald and M. O'Sullivan (Eds.), *The Handbook of Physical Education* (pp. 326–346). London, UK: Sage.

Ennis, C.D. (1999). Creating culturally relevant curriculum for disengaged girls. *Sport, Education and Society, 4*, 31–49. DOI: 10.1080/1357332990040103

Ennis, C.D., Solomon, M.A., Satina, B., Loftus, S.J., Mensch, J. and McCauley, M.T. (1999). Creating a sense of family in urban schools using the "Sport for Peace" curriculum. *Research Quarterly for Exercise and Sport, 70*, 273–285. DOI: 10.1080/02701367.1999.10608046

Enright, E. and O'Sullivan, M. (2010a). "Can I do it in my pyjamas?" Negotiating a physical education curriculum with teenage girls. *European Physical Education Review, 16*, 203–222. DOI: 10.1177/1356336X10382967

Enright, E. and O'Sullivan, M. (2010b). "Carving a new order of experience" with young people in physical education: Participatory action research as a pedagogy of possibility. In M. O'Sullivan and A. MacPhail (Eds.), *Young people's voices in physical education and youth sport*, (pp. 163–185). London, UK: Routledge.

Enright, E. and O'Sullivan M. (2012a). Physical education "In all sorts of corners": Student activists transgressing formal physical education curricular boundaries. *Research Quarterly for Exercise and Sport 83*, 255–267. DOI: 10.1080/02701367.2012.10599856

Enright, E. and O'Sullivan, M. (2012b). Producing different knowledge and producing knowledge differently: Rethinking physical education research and practice through participatory visual methods. *Sport, Education and Society, 17*, 35–55. DOI: 10.1080/13573322.2011.607911

Fisette, J. (2010). Getting to know your students. *Journal of Physical Education and Dance, 81*(7), 42–49. DOI: 10.1080/07303084.2010.10598508.

Fisette, J.L. (2011a). Exploring how girls navigate their embodied identities in physical education. *Physical Education and Sport Pedagogy, 16*, 179–196. DOI: 10.1080/17408989.2010.535199

Fisette, J.L. (2011b). Negotiating power within high school girls' exploratory projects in physical education. *Women in Sport and Physical Activity Journal, 20*, 73–90.

Fisette, J.L. and Walton, T.A. (2014). "If you really knew me" ... I am empowered through action. *Sport, Education and Society,* 131–152. DOI:10.1080/13573322.2011.643297

Fitzgerald, H. and Jobling, A. (2004). Student-centered research: Working with disabled students. In J. Wright, L. Burrows and D. Macdonald (Eds.*) Critical inquiry and problem-solving in physical education* (pp. 74–92) London, UK: Routledge.

Fletcher, S. (1984). *Women first: The female tradition in English physical education 1880–1980*. London, UK: Althone.

Freire, P. (1997). *Pedagogy of the Oppressed*. Continuum: New York, NY.

Glasby, T. and Macdonald, D. (2004). Negotiating the curriculum: Challenging the social relationships in teaching. In J. Wright, D. Macdonald and L. Burrows, (Eds.), *Critical Inquiry and Problem-solving in Physical Education* (pp.133–144). London, UK: Routledge.

Graham, G. (1995). Physical education through students' eyes and in students' voices: Introduction. *Journal of Teaching in Physical Education, 14*, 364–371.

Greene, M. (1995). *Releasing the imagination: Essays on education, the arts, and social change*. San Francisco, CA: Jossey-Bass Publishers.

Hastie, P. (1998). The participation and perceptions of girls within a unit of sport education. *Journal of Teaching in Physical Education*, 17: 157–171.

Hastie, P. and Siedentop, D. (1999). An ecological perspective on physical education. *European Physical Education Review, 5*, 9–30. DOI: 0.1177/1356336X990051002

Hellison, D. (1996). Teaching personal and social responsibility in physical education. In S. Silverman and C.D. Ennis (Eds). Student learning in physical education: Applying research to enhance instruction (pp. 269–286). Champaign, IL: Human Kinetics.

Kinchin, G.D. and O'Sullivan, M. (2003). Incidences of student support for and resistance to a curricular innovation in high school physical education. *Journal of Teaching in Physical Education, 22*, 245–260.

Lee, A., Carter, J.-A. and Xiang, P. (1995) Children's conceptions of ability in physical education. *Journal of Teaching in Physical Education* 14, 384–393.

Mitra, D.L. (2004). The significance of students: Can increasing "student voice" in schools lead to gains in youth development? *Teachers College Record, 106*(4), 651–688.

Nilges, L. (2004). Ice can look like glass: A phenomenological investigation of movement meaning in one fifth-grade creative dance unit. *Research Quarterly for Exercise and Sport*, 75: 298–314.

O'Sullivan, M. and MacPhail, A. (Eds.). (2010). *Young People's Voices in Physical Education and Youth Sport.* London, UK: Routledge.

Oldfather, P. (Ed.) (2002). Learning from student voices. *Theory into Practice, 43*(2), 67–73.

Oliver, K.L. (2010). The body, physical activity and inequity: Learning to listen *with* girls *through* action. In M. O'Sullivan and A. MacPhail (Eds.), *Young people's voices in physical education and youth sport* (pp. 31–48). London, UK: Routledge.

Oliver, K.L. and Hamzeh, M. (2010). "The boys won't let us play": 5th grade *Mestizas* publicly challenge physical activity discourse at school. *Research Quarterly for Exercise and Sport, 81*, 39–51. DOI: 10.1080/02701367.2010.10599626

Oliver, K.L., Hamzeh, M. and McCaughtry, N. (2009). "Girly girls *can* play games/*las niñas pueden jugar tambien*": Co-creating a curriculum of possibilities with 5th grade girls. *Journal of Teaching in Physical Education, 28*, 90–110.

Oliver, K.L. and Lalik, R. (2004). Critical inquiry on the body in girls' physical education classes: A critical poststructural analysis. *Journal of Teaching in Physical Education 23*, 162–195.

Oliver, K.L. and Oesterreich, H.A. (2013). Student-centred inquiry as curriculum as a model for field-based teacher education. *Journal of Curriculum Studies, 45*, 394–417.

Oliver, K.L. and Oesterreich, H.A. *with* R. Aranda, J. Archuleta, C. Blazer, K. De La Cruz, D. Martinez, J. McConnell, M. Osta, L. Parks and R. Robinson. (2015). "The sweetness of struggle": Innovation in PETE through student-centred inquiry *as* curriculum in a physical education methods course. *Physical Education and Sport Pedagogy 20*(1), 97–115. DOI: 10.1080/17408989.2013.803527

Pope, C.C. and Grant, B.C. (1996). Student experiences in sport education. *Waikato Journal of Education, 2,* 103–118.

Portman, P. (1995). Who is having fun in physical education classes? Experiences of sixth grade students in elementary and middle schools. *Journal of Teaching in Physical Education, 14*, 445–453.

Rogers, C.R. (2002). Voices inside schools: Seeing student learning: Teacher change and the role of reflection. *Harvard Educational Review, 72*, 230–253.

Rudduck, J. and McIntyre, D. (2007). *Improving learning through consulting pupils*. London, UK: Routledge.

Sanders, S. and Graham, G. (1995). Kindergarten children's initial experiences in physical education: The relentless persistence for play classes with the zone of acceptable responses. *Journal of Teaching in Physical Education, 14*, 365–372.

Schultz, K. (2003). *Listening: A Framework for teaching Across differences*. New York, NY: Teachers College Press.

Suomi, J., Collier, D. and Brown, L. (2003). Factors affecting the social experiences of students in elementary physical education classes. *Journal of Teaching in Physical Education, 22*, 186–202.

Theberge, N. (1985). Towards a feminist alternative to sport as the male preserve. *Quest 37*, 193–202. DOI: 10.1080/00336297.1985.10483834

Tjeerdsma, S., Rink, J. and Graham, K. (1996). Student perceptions, values, and beliefs prior to, during, and after badminton instruction. *Journal of Teaching in Physical Education*, 15: 464–476.

Van der Mars, H. (2006). Time and learning in physical education. In D. Kirk, D. Macdonald and M. O'Sullivan (Eds.), *The Handbook of Physical Education* (pp. 191–213). London, UK: Sage.

Veal, M.L. and Compagnone, N. (1995). How sixth graders perceive effort and skill. *Journal of Teaching in Physical Education,14*, 431–444.

Walling, M.D. and Martinek, T.J. (1995). Learned helplessness: A case study of a middle school student. *Journal of teaching in physical education, 14,* 454–466.

Wehmeyer, M. and Sands, D. (eds) (1998) *Making It Happen: Student Involvement in Educational Planning*. Baltimore, MD: Paul H Brookes Pub Co.

Youens, B. and Hall, C. (2006). Incorporating pupil perspectives in initial teacher education: Lessons from the Pupil Mentor Project. *Teacher Development*, *10*(2), 197–206.

Chapter 4

Pedagogies of Embodiment

> "I hope that my body doesn't change; I like my body. I hope that when I put on my bellbottom outfit on Thursday people will like it. I hope that if they don't, I will still be happy. I hope that I can learn to just not care what people think about my body." *Nicole, age 13*
>
> Oliver and Lalik, 2001, p. 317

> "Given that we live in a culture that uses images of beauty as a means of controlling women, the body becomes a site for political struggles. Wolf writes, 'The ideology of beauty is the last one remaining of the old feminine ideologies that still has the power to control those women whom second wave feminism would have otherwise made relatively uncontrollable' (1991 pp. 10–11). For women of color this beauty myth is doubly dangerous for the 'universal standard of beauty' sustains white supremacist images as the ideal (hooks, 1995)."
>
> Oliver, 2001, p. 145

Introduction

Centralizing embodiment pedagogically is a second critical element for working with girls from an activist perspective (Enright and O'Sullivan, 2010a; 2010b; 2012a; Fisette 2011a; 2011b; Goodyear, Casey and Kirk, 2013; Hills, 2007; Oliver, 2013; Oliver and Lalik, 2001; 2004a; Oliver, Hamzeh and McCaughtry, 2009; Oliver and Hamzeh, 2010). These activist studies support the repeated and varied calls across the past twenty-five years from physical education scholars that issues of embodiment are pertinent to our understandings of working with girls in physical education settings

(Azzarito and Katzew, 2010; Azzarito and Solmon, 2009; Azzarito and Sterling, 2010; Fisette, 2011a; Hills, 2006; 2007; Kirk and Tinning, 1994; Oliver and Lalik, 2001; Vertinsky, 1992; Wright, 1995). These studies also reflect the calls from feminists of colour that understanding embodied intersectionalities is imperative for any educational reform that seeks to enact a social justice agenda (Anzaldúa, 2007; Bordo, 1993; Butler, 1993; Collins, 1990; 1998; Delgado-Bernal, 2002; Fine, 1992; hooks, 1995; Lather, 1991; Ladson-Billings and Tate 1995; St. Pierre, 2000; Weedon, 1997; Weiler, 1988).

In the first section of this chapter we chronicle how physical education scholars have written about issues of embodiment as they relate to young people's engagement in physical education over the past several decades (Armour, 1999; Azzarito and Solmon, 2006; 2009; Evans, 2006; Garrett, 2004; Hills, 2007; Kirk and Tinning, 1994; McDermott, 2000; Oliver and Lalik, 2000; 2001; Satina and Hultgren, 2001; Velija and Kumar, 2009; Vertinsky, 1992). We will show that although there is a good deal of discussion about embodiment and its importance, there is no clear and consistent way in which different scholars use the term embodiment. Nonetheless there is a relative consistency in the claims that embodiment is important to our understandings of young people and their engagements and disengagements in physical education and physical activity participation (c.f., Azzarito and Katzew, 2010; Enright and O'Sullivan, 2010a; Kirk and Tinning, 1994; Oliver, 2001; Vertinsky, 1992).

In the second part of the chapter we discuss how activist scholars have given embodiment a pedagogical form. Centred *in* concrete pedagogical projects about how to engage girls in the process of critically studying issues of embodiment, this research has moved beyond abstract and theoretical discussions *about* the value of girls' embodiment (Fisette 2011a; Oliver, 2001; Enright and O'Sullivan, 2013). Drawing on feminist, poststructural and critical theories (Davies, 2000; Fine, 1994; Freire, 1974; 1985; Giroux, 1997; hooks, 1990; Ladson-Billings and Tate, 1995; Luke and Gore, 1992; Shannon, 1990; Shor, 1992; Weedon, 1997; Weiler, 1988), collectively, activists work from the stance that until girls can name the forms of inequities that contribute to how they are learning to think and feel about their bodies and physical activity, educators will not have the necessary knowledge with which to assist girls in the process of coming to value the physically active life.

Embodiment and physical education

In 1992 Vertinsky wrote of the need for 'gender-sensitive' physical education:

> Teachers ... would do well to encourage girls to talk about their bodies, how they feel about their sizes and shapes, and the different ways their bodies can move. These views of the body can then be discussed in terms of dominant messages that girls get about their bodies in this culture... *An approach to physical education that emphasizes agency, action and the possibility of transformation* [emphasis added] and focuses on more than the single attainment of target of physical activity (pp. 389–390).

Vertinsky's ground-breaking work laid a foundation for physical education scholars to start paying closer attention to how issues of embodiment influence girls' lives. The notion of embodiment has been used in the gender literature in physical education since at least the late 1980s, though its use has been patchy in several respects. Where the term embodiment is used, it is rarely defined in any direct way (for example, Velija and Kumar, 2009). In contrast, although the term is sometimes mentioned infrequently (Vertinsky, 1992) or not at all (Wright and King, 1990), it is clear that authors in and out of physical education have much to say on embodiment and it's centrality to girls' lives.

From the late 1980s to the early 2000s, scholars wrote of the historical and philosophical debilitating mind/body dualism that created the backdrop for culture to disembody and objectify human beings and, in particular, women (Dewey, 1922; Satina and Hultgren, 2001). As such, scholars (Theberge, 1991; Vertinsky, 1992; hooks, 1995) began describing how women's sense of self is disrupted when the female body is objectified and demeaned in society. Theoretical arguments continued to filter through the literature on how the body is used as a means of regulating people's behaviours (Bordo, 1989; 1985; Kirk, 1998; Shilling, 1993; Sparkes, 1996; 1997; Wright, 2000). In particular, feminists began documenting how the body plays a crucial role in the reciprocal relationship between women's private and public identities and offered critiques of how women's bodies are used within culture to continue the oppression of girls and women (Bloom and Munro, 1995) with particular emphases on race (Anzaldúa, 2007; Collins,

1990; 1998; hooks, 1989; 1990; 1995; Fordham, 1996; Oliver and Lalik, 2000), on social class (Collins, 1990; Oliver, 1999), on gender (Bordo, 1989; 1997; Wolf, 1991; Oliver and Lalik, 2001), on sexuality (Fine, 1993), and on age and ability (Fitzgerald, 2009; Sparkes, 1997). What became increasingly clear during this period of time was not *what* was important with respects to embodiment, but *that* embodiment was indeed central to our understandings of girls and their engagements with physical culture.

Looking back at this body of literature we note a number of terms related to embodiment that scholars in physical education research use. These include, for example, embodied identities (Kirk and Tinning, 1994), embodied subjectivities (Wright, 1995), body-narratives (Oliver, 1999), physicality (McDermott, 2000), habitus (Gorely, Holroyd and Kirk, 2003), body-meanings (Azzarito, Solmon and Harrison, 2006), physical self (Crocker et al., 2006), and the embodiment of gender (Velija and Kumar, 2009). Despite the lack of consistent terminology over the years, and an apparent reluctance to define the term within physical education, there is much consistency in the literature around the importance of girls' embodiment in physical education and related contexts.

With respect to the importance of embodiment for girls, all of this work, without exception, either implicitly or explicitly, takes an anti-dualist stance (Dewey, 1922). In an early contribution drawing on phenomenology and existentialism, Whitehead (1990) claimed that every human is an indivisible whole and that embodiment and personhood are inseparable. Satina and Hultgren (2001) similarly note (quoting Heidegger) that "We do not 'have' a body; rather, we 'are' bodily" (p. 521). They go on to charge that Cartesian dualism not only separates body and mind, but also devalues the body while privileging the intellect. In so doing, they argue, the body is objectified as a thing and only to be understood as an object through scientific discourses. In her critique of this dualist tendency in education, Whitehead (2010) argued that the body-as-lived is "the ongoing axis of thought and knowing" and is thus of primary importance in education (p. 26).

Building on this monist perspective, several authors within physical education have provided insights into what Young (1980) called "the *situation* of being a woman in a particular society" (p. 140). Young argued against the prevailing wisdom of the time in motor development research with young children that despite evidence of a "more or less typical style of running like a girl, climbing like a girl, swinging like a girl, hitting like a girl", this distinctively female way of moving is not due to some "feminine essence" but, rather, is learned. In a patriarchal social order, women learn to move in a confined field because they learn that "feminine bodily existence is self-referred to the extent that the feminine subject posits her motion as the motion that is *looked at*" (p. 148, original emphasis).

Other authors have developed Young's notion of the situation of being a woman in relation to school physical education and other organized physical activity. For example, Wright and King (1990) note that there is considerable ambiguity surrounding girls' engagements with physical education. On the one hand, girls are "constructed by patriarchal discourses of femininity that work to constrain and restrain their behaviour", but on the other hand, in physical education lessons "they are expected to be active, competitive, and achievement-oriented" (p. 222). The net effect, according to Wright and King, is that conventional ways of being feminine consistently undermine expectations in physical education regarding "activity, achievement and effort" and reproduce the gender relations of the wider society.

Vertinsky (1992) supports Wright and King's analysis and notes that part of the source of the contradictions girls experience in physical education is that they are compared unfavourably in co-educational settings. Here, the male standard is used as the norm thereby portraying girls "as 'deficient' males or passive victims of restrictive gender-stereotyped attitudes and practices" (p. 328). Similarly, Wright (1995) has argued that the male standard as norm is manifest in the dominance of team games traditionally associated with males, while activities traditionally associated with females such as dance are viewed as marginal within the physical education curriculum. Echoing Young, Vertinsky (1992) sums up the situation of girls in physical education, where they learn "to experience their bodies as fragile encumbrances, as objects and burdens, rather than as living manifestations of action and intention. As a consequence, many readily learned to underestimate their bodily capacity for sport and games" (p. 375).

Vertinsky (1992) recognized the need for a different approach to physical education in order to address these ambiguities and contradictions that characterize the situation of girls. As we noted at the beginning of the section, she argued the need for a "gender sensitive" physical education. Several scholars have echoed her call for educators to create curricular opportunities for girls to name and critique the patriarchal discourses surrounding their embodiment. Armour (1999) argued that as physical education is "body-focused", physical educators should make this focus explicit as their subject "can have a major role to play in the establishment of pupils' embodied identity" (p. 10). Satina and Hultgren (2001) argued for the development of a "pedagogy of embodiment" that offers girls opportunities to "develop and express self-affirming views of their body in an atmosphere that does not replicate culturally imposed limitations" (p. 530). Drawing on an activist project of working with girls in physical education, Oliver and Lalik (2001) developed the notion of the "body-as-curriculum", explaining that they "wanted to develop a curriculum of the body that would begin with girls' experiences, interests and concerns with their bodies, rather than featuring adults' perspectives exclusively" (p. 307). Further studies have added support to these calls to create gender-sensitive forms of physical education, with Gorely, Holroyd and Kirk (2003) and Azzarito, Solmon and Harrison (2006) arguing "a 'gender-relevant' critical pedagogy should be employed in physical education classes to offer alternative constructions of embodied femininities and masculinities" (p. 97), while Crocker et al. (2006) advocate "interventions focused on the physical self and body image need to target young adolescents, if not children" (p. 197).

The possibilities for creating alternative forms of physical education, according to these scholars, must address the notion of using the male standard as the norm thereby positioning girls as "deficient" males (Vertinsky, 1992). This issue is part of the wider gender order of society. With respect to embodiment, Bourdieu (2001) has noted that when we come to consider masculine domination, we must account not only for the social and economic circumstances in societies that favour men over women, but the embedding of these social structures in the body itself. He writes, "the masculinisation of the male body and the feminization of the female body, immense and in a sense interminable tasks ... induce a somatization of the relations of domination, which is thus naturalized" (pp. 55–56). This somatization of the relations of domination is a matter of fundamental importance to physical educators, as it suggests socially-critical working on and with the body must be part of any process of improving social equality (Wright and King, 1990; Vertinsky, 1992). In this context, Bourdieu (2001) states:

> [the] intensive practice of a sport leads to a profound transformation of the subjective and objective experience of the body. It no longer exists only for others or ... for the mirror... Instead of being a body for others it becomes a body for oneself; the passive body becomes an active and acting body. (p. 67)

Bourdieu notes that the power of masculine domination is such that women who play sport take many risks, including having their femininity and sexuality called into question. But these risks precisely make his point; the subversion of the gender order through an active and acting body provokes strong reactions in some men and women as it appears that the "natural order of things" itself is being brought into question.

Indeed, the ways in which girls as active and acting embodied beings might practice the physically active life is differentiated according to private and public spaces (Markula, 1995). Azzarito and Sterling (2010), in a study of minority ethnic girls in England, noted that public spaces were seen by the girls to be male spaces and therefore fraught with risk as there they were subject to "the gaze", and their preferences for physical activity were overwhelmingly in the private space of home. Although we have noted the unfavourable comparison of girls to the male standard as norm, we might also consider along with Hills (2007) that these standards operate even in girl-only physical education environments, and that girl-only spaces are not necessarily safer for less-skilled girls if they lack social status or a friendship group. Moreover, Evans (2006) claims that along with peer scrutiny and criticism, "the evaluative gaze of the teachers exerts power over the pupils, intensifying the gaze and other comments from peers (fear of ridicule), and also self-criticism (fear of inadequacy)" (p. 557).

Collectively what this literature suggests unequivocally is that a pedagogy of embodiment is key to the development of forms of physical education that better meet girls' needs. At the same time, Vertinsky (1992) argued "it is unlikely that one single approach will serve the interests of all girls—in all sporting contexts... A gender-sensitive perspective is thus one that lets patterns of discrimination themselves determine what action to take to eliminate bias" (p. 383). We consider this comment to be underpinned by a pragmatist perspective that, as we noted in Chapter 1, asks how might we improve the situation for girls in physical education? Although there is no one-size-fits-all answer to this question, the literature would suggest that creating spaces for girls to study embodiment is a critical element in physical education.

Embodiment within an activist approach

> "That's sick... Too muscular... I just think women should be feminine ... not where you can see the muscle cause I think that's masculine." *Alysa, age 13*
>
> Oliver 1999, 239

Feminist authors (Bordo, 1989; Collins, 1990; hooks, 1995; Vertinsky, 1992; Wolf, 1991) claim that the "body plays a crucial role in the reciprocal relationship between women's private and public identities. The social meanings publicly attached to the body can become internalized and exert powerful influences on women's private feelings of self-worth" (Oliver and Lalik, 2001, p. 305). Alongside student-centred pedagogy, a second key feature of activist work involved in engaging adolescent girls in physical education involves teachers creating spaces in their curriculum for girls to critically explore their embodiment (for example, Enright and O'Sullivan, 2013; Goodyear, Casey and Kirk 2013; Hamzeh 2012; Oliver and Lalik 2001; 2004a). A pedagogy of embodiment helps girls "name the discourses that shape their lives and regulate their bodies ... [in order to support] girls' efforts to develop strategies for identifying, resisting, and disrupting forms of enculturation that threaten their health and limit their life chances" (Oliver and Lalik, 2004a, 162–163). These studies, as well as other's work on girls' embodiment (for example, Azzarito and Solmon 2009; Hills 2006; Garrett 2004) provide strong evidence that although purposeful physical activity is necessary to girls' engagements in physical education, it is not sufficient by itself. Offering girls the opportunities to explore their embodiment is central to creating relevant physical education for girls.

In working towards understanding how to centralize girls' embodiment pedagogically, activist scholars in physical education have consistently approached their work with girls from an anti-dualist stance, have actively sought ways to help girls name experiences of their bodies that are often at a pre-conscious level in order for girls to be able to reflect on those experiences critically, and worked to support girls' sense of physicality in movement.

Activists' work with embodied pedagogies disrupts the debilitating mind-body dualism that privileges and values the mind while objectifying the body as something to be controlled, manipulated, and "looked at" (Dewey, 1922; Grumet, 1988; hooks, 1995). This mind/body dualism too often plagues our systems of education (Dewey, 1922; Garrison, 1997; Kirk, 1992), our pedagogical practices (Satina and Hultgren, 2001) and our traditional physical education curricula (Oliver and Garrison, 1996; Wright, 1995). Starting from the perspective that *how* girls experience their bodies underpins their learning, activists have intentionally sought to make girls' bodies central in their curricula (Enright and O'Sullivan, 2010a; Fisette, 2011a; Oliver, 1999; 2001; Oliver and Lalik, 2000; 2001; 2004a). Placing the body at the centre disrupts the mind/body dualism of traditional practice thereby creating the cracks necessary for better understanding how girls read, internalize, resist, or reject forms and processes of oppression that threaten their health as well as their abilities, interests, and willingness to learn to value the physically active life. These cracks also create the spaces for better understanding girls' hopes; spaces not only for the language of critique but also the language of possibility (Fine, 1994). In this context, Giroux (1997) writes:

> A critical pedagogy has to begin with a dialectical celebration of the languages of critique and possibility—an approach which finds its noblest expressions in a discourse integrating critical analysis with social transformation [around] problems rooted in the concrete experiences of everyday life. (p. 132)

As activists have made girls' everyday experiences of their bodies central to physical education (Enright and O'Sullivan, 2010a; Fisette, 2011a; Oliver and Lalik, 2001; Oliver, Hamzeh and McCaughtry, 2009), they have come to understand the circulating discourses that shape girls' subjectivities, have been able to search for places to explore girls' agency, and have worked collaboratively with girls to practice change (Davies, 2000; Weis and Fine, 2004; Weedon, 1997). The results have been a much clearer understanding of *how* girls experience their bodies through dominant cultural narratives that objectify and demean girls' bodies, as well as *how* and *where* they resist these same oppressive narratives, and *how* they identify what they want to change (Fisette, 2011a; Oliver and Lalik, 2001; 2004a). Fisette (2011a) and Oliver and Hamzeh's (2010) work illustrates this point:

> I don't like sexist things ... the whole female ball thing that really annoys me even though they are easier to throw. It's just the whole point that he's making us think that we can't throw the bigger ones... I think if he puts them out, he shouldn't call them female balls, just be like, 'Here's smaller ones, throw them if you want. Anyone can throw them'.
>
> Fisette, 2011a, p. 13

> Kim: Marie you said that sometimes the boys won't let the girls play because they have the wrong color of skin and they had taken a picture of you [Maggie Mae]...
> Maggie Mae: Yeah ... they told me I couldn't play because I was a girl and I was Black... Sometimes I know that at the fifth-grade recess, some of the boys don't want the girls to play because they are girls, and I think that is a problem because we should all be able to do what we want to do; we should be able to play what we want to play.
>
> Oliver and Hamzeh, 2010, p. 43

A second way that activist scholars have worked with embodied pedagogies is by actively seeking ways to help girls name their experiences of their bodies that are often at a pre-conscious level. Greene (1995) writes:

> Only when the taken-for-granted is subject to questioning, only when we take various, sometimes unfamiliar perspectives on it, does it show itself as what it is—contingent on many interpretations, many vantage points, unified (if at all) by conformity or by unexamined common sense. Once we can see our givens as contingencies, then we may have the opportunity to posit alternative ways of living and valuing and to make choices. (p. 23)

Part of what activist scholars have consistently done is to find ways to help girls name the meanings of their bodily experiences. An example from Oliver's (2001) work is this task: "Go through the magazines and cut out pictures and/or text that are of interest to you and categorize your pictures/text any way you want" (p. 148). Many of the findings from activist work have come only after using creative methods such as this for assisting girls to find ways to put language to experiences that are difficult to explain in part because so many of these experiences operate on a pre-conscious level. Visual methodologies such as magazine explorations and critiques (Oliver and Lalik, 2000; 2001; 2004a; Enright and O'Sullivan, 2013), photographic inquiry (Oliver and Lalik, 2004a; 2004b; Oliver, Hamzeh and McCaughtry, 2009; Oliver and Hamzeh, 2010), photographic essays (Oliver and Lalik, 2004a), scrap-booking (Enright and O'Sullivan, 2010a; 2012b; Hamzeh, 2012), mapping (Enright and O'Sullivan, 2010a; Hamzeh and Oliver, 2012; Oliver, 1999), and drawing (Oliver, 1999; Fisette, 2014) have all been methods that activists have used to assist girls in the process of naming issues that influence their embodiment.

In addition to using visual methods as a means for girls to put language to experience, activist scholars have also used a variety of techniques to help girls further elaborate experiences that are only partially explained. For example, asking girls to imagine a world where particular things no longer existed (i.e., people didn't care how they looked, there was no such thing as "normal" female behaviour, there was no longer racism) was found useful in helping girls better describe the circumstances with which they currently experienced their bodies (Oliver, 1999). Asking girls to talk about what "other girls" might think about their bodies was another technique useful in creating public settings where girls would talk about issues of embodiment that were important to them (for example, anorexia and bulimia, teen pregnancy).

Through the process of trying to assist girls to find ways to name experiences that influence their embodiment so that they can start to look at these experiences from a variety of vantage points (Greene, 1995), what activists have learned is that this process takes time, patience, and creativity. Girls need multiple opportunities for exploring their embodiment because it is through these multiple and varied opportunities that they are able to better articulate what they know and feel. For example, in Oliver's (2001) work, 13-year-old African American girls were writing about the magazine images they had selected as a way to represent messages that girls receive about their bodies. One of the girls, Alexandria, looked up and said:

> 'I have a concept I want to talk about.' She went on to explain that, 'some girls at our school are pregnant'. The group began discussing how they were curious to know what it 'felt like to be pregnant' and how important it was to have their

> 'mothers' to talk with because 'they don't talk about it [teen pregnancy] at school'. Brandi mentioned that when they were in 5th grade they saw a film but that 'then most people didn't have questions and everyone was too embarrassed to ask questions'. She continued by saying, 'Now everybody got all these questions and there ain't nobody to ask.'
>
> Oliver, 2001, p. 160

This is only one of many types of conversations activists have had in their work with girls. What is important about assisting girls to name their experiences is that adults can begin to better understand just how important girls' embodiment is to their interest in learning to be healthy adults.

Another way activist scholars have worked towards understanding how to centralize girls' embodiment pedagogically is through their supporting and nurturing girls' sense of physicality in movement. What is pivotal to the success of such endeavours was these scholars' willingness to support girls' physicality on the girls' terms, rather than on some preconceived adult notion of "what should be". Here is where we see how girls' notions of embodiment lie beneath the surface. To illustrate our point we use an example from a study by Oliver and her colleagues (Oliver, Hamzeh and McCaughtry, 2009). In 2005–2006 Oliver worked with two groups of 10–11-year-old Mexican American, Hispanic and White 5th grade girls in a poor, rural border community about 40 minutes from Juarez, Mexico. The girls were selected to work with Oliver one day per week for the entire school year by their physical education teacher. The teacher labelled these girls as either not liking physical education or not liking physical activity in general. The study aimed to work with these girls to help them identify barriers to their physical activity enjoyment and participation and work with them to negotiate the barriers within their control so as to increase their opportunities for engaging in physical activity.

The girls were given cameras at the beginning of the study and asked to photograph things that helped them be physically active and things that either prevented them from being active or prevented them from enjoying physical activity. Through this process the girls explained that being a "girly girl" often prevented them from being physically active because girly girls "don't want to sweat", "mess up their hair and nails", they didn't want to "mess up their nice clothes" and sometimes they liked to wear "flip flops".

What Oliver began to learn as time went on was that these girls were using the idea of "being a girly girl" as an excuse for not engaging in physical education. Over time they started to talk about how when the teacher was having them play something they didn't like such as football, soccer, basketball and Frisbee that they used excuses such as "we don't want to sweat" or "we don't want to mess up our clothes" as a way of getting out of the activity that wasn't meeting their particular needs. Below is a conversation Oliver had with the girls as they were explaining why they didn't like these sports:

> Maltilde says, 'because the boys kick your feet,' 'trip you on purpose,' 'push you down,' 'they won't give you the ball,' and 'grab your hair.' So I asked them whether it was the sport they didn't like or the way that sport was being played. I said, 'So if the boys are kicking you or tripping you or pulling your hair or not giving you the ball those kinds of things...' Sunshine cut me off and says, 'You feel left out and hurt.' I continued, 'I'm trying to figure out, if there are a lot of girls that are girly girls or identify as girly girls, they should be able to be active in ways that are...' Sunshine cuts me off again and says, 'Suitable for them.' I continue, 'Yes, that are suitable, wouldn't you think?' ... Sunshine goes on to explain that if girls 'felt comfortable with themselves they would be able to do physical activity'.
>
> Oliver, Hamzeh and McCaughtry, 2009, p. 102

What Oliver came to better understand from these girls was that not only did they not like the content in physical education – the traditional team sports – but they also did not like how the activities were played when boys were involved, did not like getting hurt or being left out, and wanted to be able to play and "feel comfortable with themselves". So, rather than play in situations they identified as unsuitable or dangerous, they chose not to participate. What is so concerning here is that because their excuses of "not wanting to sweat or mess up their clothes" are SUCH normalized discourses around girls disengagement in physical education, no one questioned whether there might be some other reason they didn't want to play.

Rather than try to get the girls to critique how the notion of "girly girl" was contributing to their disengagement, Oliver suggested that they work collaboratively to negotiate their barriers by making up games girls could play while simultaneously being a "girly girl". So what they did was to create a book for games for days the girls "didn't want to sweat" or "didn't want to mess up their clothes", "break a nail", "didn't want to mess up their hair", and days that they wore flip flops. Through the process of Oliver working to support these girls' physicality of movement on their terms what started to happen was that the content of the games they created contradicted many of their self-identified girly girl barriers. That is, although they may have been making up games for days where they did not want to sweat or mess up their nice clothes, many of the actual games involved running, jumping, chasing, and fleeing, the possibility of sweating or getting their clothes dirty. Take, for example, run-around kickball. The girls created this game for the days they didn't want to mess up their nice clothes. It involved kicking a ball, then the team that kicked all ran the bases while the outfielders collected the ball and chased the girls running the bases trying to catch them. This study was conducted in a desert community, thus they played the game in the dust so the possibility of the girls messing up their clothes was pretty certain. Many of their games had these types of contradictions. What Oliver learned was that if we want girls to learn to value the physically active life we need to start from where girls *are*, and assist them in finding activities that *they* find valuable and relevant and enjoyable, regardless of what we think. This example highlights just how central girls' embodiment is to their physical activity participation and that we cannot trivialize or dismiss this centrality if we hope to assist girls in becoming physically active for life.

Conclusion

In this chapter we have highlighted that despite a lack of conceptual consistency in the literature about issues of embodiment, what comes through as essential is the unequivocal agreement of its importance in the lives of girls. Part of this discussion has included the calls for researchers and teachers to create opportunities for girls to critically reflect on how issues of embodiment influence their lives. This research has created the context from which activists have worked to centralize embodiment pedagogically with girls. In doing so they have worked from an anti-dualist stance, have actively sought ways to help girls name experiences of their bodies that are often at a pre-conscious level in order for girls to be able to reflect on those experiences critically, and worked to support girls' sense of physicality in movement.

These processes have emerged in part from a student-centred approach to working with girls. In the next chapter we will show how student-centred pedagogy and critical study of embodiment merge to form a basis from which inquiry-oriented approaches to learning create spaces for teachers and students to take action; action designed at better facilitating girls engagement, learning and enjoyment in physical education and physical activity.

References

Anzaldúa, G. (2007). *Borderlands/La frontera: The new mestiza* (3rd ed.). San Francisco, CA: Aunt Lute Books.

Armour, K.M. (1999). The case for a body-focus in education and physical education. *Sport, Education and Society, 4*, 5–15. DOI: 10.1080/1357332990040101

Azzarito, L.M. and Katzew, A. (2010). Performing identities in physical education: (En)gendering fluid selves. *Research Quarterly for Exercise and Sport, 81*, 25–37. DOI: 10.1080/02701367.2010.10599625

Azzarito, L.M. and Solmon, M.A. (2006). A poststructural analysis of high school students' gendered and racialized bodily meanings. *Journal of Teaching in Physical Education, 25*, 75–98.

Azzarito, L,M. and Solmon, M.A. (2009). An investigation of students' embodied discourses in physical education: A gendered project. *Journal of Teaching in Physical Education, 28*, 173–191.

Azzarito, L.M., Solmon, M.A. and Harrison, L. (2006). "...If I had a choice, I would..." A feminist post-structural perspective on girls in physical education. *Research Quarterly for Exercise and Sport, 77*, 222–239. DOI: 10.1080/02701367.2006.10599356

Azzarito, L.M. and Sterling J. (2010). "What It Was in my Eyes": Picturing youths' embodiment in "real" spaces. *Qualitative Research in Sport and Exercise, 2*(2), 209–228. DOI: 10.1080/19398441.2010.488029

Bloom, L.R. and Munro, P. (1995). Conflicts of selves: Nonunitary subjectivity in women administrators' life history narratives. In J.A Hatch and R. Wisniewski (Eds.), *Life history and narrative* (pp. 99–112). Washington, DC: Falmer Press.

Bordo, S.R. (1989).The body and the reproduction of femininity: A feminist appropriation of Foucault, in A.M. Jaggar and S.R. Bordo

(Eds.), *Gender/Body/Knowledge: Feminist reconstructions of being and knowing*. (pp. 18–33). New Brunswick, NJ: Rutgers University Press.

Bordo, S.R. (1993). *Unbearable weight: Feminism, western culture, and the body*. Berkeley, CA: University of California Press.

Bordo, S.R. (1997) The body and the reproduction of femininity, in: K. Conboy, N. Medina and S. Stanbury (Eds.), *Writing on the body: Female embodiment and feminist theory* (pp. 90–110). New York: Columbia University Press.

Bourdieu, P. (2001). *Masculine Domination*. Cambridge, UK: Polity.

Butler, J. (1993). *Bodies that matter: On the discursive limits of sex*. New York, NY: Routledge.

Collins, P.H. (1990). Black feminist thought: Knowledge, consciousness, and the politics of empowerment, perspectives on gender. Boston, MA: Unwin Hyman.

Collins, P.H. (1998). *Fighting words: Black women and the search for justice*. Minneapolis, MN: University of Minnesota Press.

Crocker, P.R., Sabiston, C.M., Kowalski, K.C., McDonough, M.H. and Kowalski, N. (2006). Longitudinal assessment of the relationship between physical self-concept and health-related behavior and emotion in adolescent girls. *Journal of Applied Sport Psychology, 18*, 185–200. DOI: 10.1080/10413200600830257

Davies, B. (2000). *A Body of writing, 1990–1999*. New York, NY: AltaMira Press.

Delgado Bernal, D. (2002). Critical race theory, Latino critical theory, and critical raced-gendered epistemologies: Recognizing students of color as holders and creators of knowledge. *Qualitative Inquiry, 8,* 105–126. DOI: 10.1177/107780040200800107

Dewey, J. (1922) *Human nature and conduct: An introduction to social psychology*. New York: Carlton House.

Enright, E. and O'Sullivan, M. (2010a). "Can I do it in my pyjamas?" Negotiating a physical education curriculum with teenage girls. *European Physical Education Review, 16*, 203–222. DOI: 10.1177/1356336X10382967

Enright, E. and O'Sullivan, M. (2010b). "Carving a new order of experience" with young people in physical education: Participatory action research as a pedagogy of possibility. In M. O'Sullivan and A. MacPhail (Eds.), *Young people's voices in physical education and youth sport*, (pp. 163–185). London, UK: Routledge.

Enright, E. and O'Sullivan M. (2012a). Physical education "In all sorts of corners": Student activists transgressing formal physical education curricular boundaries. *Research Quarterly for Exercise and Sport 83*, 255–267. DOI: 10.1080/02701367.2012.10599856

Enright, E. and O'Sullivan, M. (2012b). Producing different knowledge and producing knowledge differently: Rethinking physical education research and practice through participatory visual methods. *Sport, Education and Society, 17*, 35–55. DOI: 10.1080/13573322.2011.607911

Enright, E, and O'Sullivan, M. (2013). "Now, I'm magazine detective the whole time": Listening and responding to young people's complex experiences of popular physical culture. *Journal of Teaching in Physical Education, 32*, 394–418.

Evans, B. (2006). "I'd feel ashamed": Girls' bodies and sports participation. *Gender, Place & Culture: A Journal of Feminist Geography, 13*, 547–561. DOI: 10.1080/09663690600858952

Fine, M. (1992). Disruptive voices: *The possibilities of feminist research.* Ann Arbor, MI: University of Michigan Press.

Fine, M. (1994). Distance and other stances: Negotiations of power inside feminist research. In A. Gitlin (Ed.), *Power and method: political activism and educational research* (pp. 13–35). New York: Routledge.

Fisette, J.L. (2011a). Exploring how girls navigate their embodied identities in physical education. *Physical Education and Sport Pedagogy, 16*, 179–196. DOI: 10.1080/17408989.2010.535199

Fisette, J.L. (2011b). Negotiating power within high school girls' exploratory projects in physical education. *Women in Sport and Physical Activity Journal, 20*, 73–90.

Fisette, J.L. (2014). Activity #18: Giving voice to the moving body through pictures and drawings. In J.K. Dowdy and K. Cushner (Eds.), *Reading between the lines: Activities for developing social awareness literacy.* (pp. 109–114). Lanham, MD: Rowman & Littlefield.

Fitzgerald, H. (ed) (2009) *Disability and Youth Sport* London, UK: Routledge.

Fordham, S. (1996). *Blacked out: Dilemmas of race, identity, and success at Capital High.* Chicago, IL: University of Chicago Press.

Foucault, M. (1985). *The history of sexuality: Vol. 2. The use of pleasure.* New York, NY: Random House.

Freire, P. (1974). *Pedagogy of the oppressed.* New York, NY: Seabury Press.

Freire, P. (1985). *The politics of education: culture, power, and liberation.* Westport, CT: Bergin & Garvey.

Garrett, R. (2004). Negotiating a physical identity: Girls, bodies and physical education. *Sport, Education and Society*, 9, 223–237. DOI: 10.1080/1357332042000233958

Garrison, J. (1997). *Dewey and Eros: Wisdom and desire in the art of teaching,* New York, NY: Teachers College Press.

Giroux, H.A. (1997). *Pedagogy and the politics of hope: Theory, culture, and schooling.* Boulder, CO: Westview Press.

Goodyear, V., Casey, A. and Kirk, D. (2013). Slights, cameras, inaction: Using flip cameras in cooperative learning to explore girls' (dis) engagment in physical education. In L. Azzarito and D. Kirk (Eds.), *Pedagogies, physical culture, and visual methods* (pp. 47–61). New York, NY: Routledge.

Gorely, T., Holroyd, R. and Kirk, D. (2003). Muscularity, the habitus and the social construction of gender: Towards a gender relevant physical education. *British Journal of Sociology of Education, 24*, 429–448. DOI: 10.1080/01425690301923

Greene, M. (1995). *Releasing the imagination: Essays on education, the arts, and social change*. San Francisco, CA: Jossey-Bass Publishers.

Grumet, M. (1988). *Bitter milk: Women and teaching*. Amherst, MA: University of Massachusetts Press.

Hamzeh, M. (2012). *Pedagogies of deveiling: Muslim girls & the hijab discourse*. Charlotte, North Carolina: Information Age Publishing, Inc.

Hamzeh, M. and K.L. Oliver. (2012). "Because I am Muslim, I cannot wear a swimsuit": Muslim girls negotiate participation opportunities for physical activity. *Research Quarterly for Exercise and Sport 83*, 330–339. DOI: 10.1080/02701367.2012.10599864

Hills, A. (2006). Playing the field(s): An exploration of change, conformity and conflict in girls' understandings of gendered physicality in physical education. *Gender and Education 18*, 539–556. DOI: 10.1080/09540250600881691

Hills, L. (2007). Friendship, physicality, and physical education: An exploration of the social and embodied dynamics of girls' physical education experiences. *Sport, Education and Society 12*, 317–336. DOI: 10.1080/13573320701464275

hooks, b. (1989). Talking back: *Thinking feminist, thinking black*. Boston, MA: South End Press.

hooks, b. (1990). *Yearning: Race, gender, and cultural politics*. Boston, MA: South End Press.

hooks, b. (1995). *Killing rage: Ending racism*. New York, NY: Henry Holt.

Kirk, D. (1992) *Defining Physical Education: the social construction of a school subject in postwar Britain*, London, UK: Falmer.

Kirk, D. (1998). *Schooling bodies: School practice and public discourse 1880–1950*. London, UK: Leicester University Press.

Kirk, D. and Tinning, R. (1994). Embodied self-identity, healthy lifestyles and school physical education. *Sociology of Health & Illness, 16*, 600–625. DOI: 10.1111/1467-9566.ep11348096

Ladson-Billings, G. and Tate, W.F. (1995). Toward a critical race theory of education. *Teachers College Record*, 97(1), 47–67.

Lather, P. (1991). Getting smart: Feminist research and pedagogy with/in the postmodern. New York, NY: Routledge.

Luke, C. and Gore, J. (1992). *Feminisms and critical pedagogy*. New York, NY: Routledge.

Markula, P. (1995). Firm but shapely, fit but sexy, strong but thin: The postmodern aerobicizing female bodies. *Sociology of Sport Journal, 12*, 424–453.

McDermott, L. (2000). A qualitative assessment of the significance of body perception to women's physical activity experiences: Revisiting discussions of physicalities. *Sociology of Sport Journal*, 17, 331–363.

O'Sullivan, M. and MacPhail, A. (Eds.). (2010). *Young People's Voices in Physical Education and Youth Sport*. London, UK: Routledge.

Oliver, K.L. (1999). Adolescent girls' body-narratives: Learning to desire and create a 'fashionable' image. *Teachers College Record, 101*(2), 220–246.

Oliver, K.L. (2001). Images of the body from popular culture: Engaging adolescent girls in critical inquiry. *Sport, Education & Society* 6, 143–164. DOI: 10.1080/13573320120084245

Oliver, K.L. (2013). Beyond words: The visual as a form of student-centered inquiry of the body and physical activity. In L. Azzarito and D. Kirk (Eds.), *Physical culture, pedagogies and visual methods* (pp. 15–29). New York, NY: Routledge.

Oliver, K.L. and Garrison, J. (1996). A narrative journey: Beyond the myth of the mind/body and self/society dualisms. *Proceedings of the Fortieth Annual Meeting of the South Atlantic Philosophy of Education Society*, pp. 55–65.

Oliver, K.L. and Hamzeh, M. (2010). "The boys won't let us play": 5th grade *Mestizas* publicly challenge physical activity discourse at school. *Research Quarterly for Exercise and Sport, 81*, 39–51. DOI: 10.1080/02701367.2010.10599626

Oliver, K.L., Hamzeh, M. and McCaughtry, N. (2009). "Girly girls *can* play games/*las niñas pueden jugar tambien*": Co-creating a curriculum of possibilities with 5th grade girls. *Journal of Teaching in Physical Education, 28*, 90–110.

Oliver, K.L. and Lalik, R. (2000). *Bodily knowledge: Learning about equity and justice with adolescent girls*. New York, NY: Peter Lang Publishing, Inc.

Oliver, K.L. and Lalik, R. (2001). The body as curriculum: Learning with adolescent girls. *The Journal of Curriculum Studies 33*, 303–333. DOI: 10.1080/00220270010006046

Oliver, K.L. and Lalik, R. (2004a). Critical inquiry on the body in girls' physical education classes: A critical poststructural analysis. *Journal of Teaching in Physical Education* 23, 162–195.

Oliver, K.L. and Lalik, R. (2004b). "The beauty walk, this ain't my topic": Learning about critical inquiry with adolescent girls. *The Journal of Curriculum Studies 36*, 555–586. DOI: 10.1080/0022027032000139397

St. Pierre, E.A. (2000). Poststructural feminism in education: An overview. *Qualitative Studies in Education, 13*, 477–515. DOI: 10.1080/09518390050156422

Satina, B. and Hultgren F. (2001). The absent body of girls made visible: Embodiment as the focus in education. *Studies in Philosophy and Education 20*, 521–534. DOI: 10.1023/A:1012286500997

Shannon, P. (1990). *The struggle to continues: Progressive reading instruction in the United States.* Portsmouth, NH: Heinemann.

Shilling, C. (1993). *The body and social theory.* London, UK: Sage.

Shor, I. (1992). *Empowering education: Critical teaching for social change.* Chicago, IL: University of Chicago Press.

Sparkes, A.C. (1996). Interrupted body projects and the self in teaching: Exploring an absent present. *International Studies in Sociology of Education* 6, 167–187. DOI: 10.1080/0962021960060203

Sparkes, A.C. (1997). Reflections on the socially constructed physical self. In K. Fox (Ed.), *The physical self: From motivation to well-being* (pp. 88–110). Champaign, IL: Human Kinetics Press.

Theberge, N. (1991). Reflection on the body in the sociology of sport. *Quest, 43*, 123–134. DOI: 10.1080/00336297.1991.10484017

Velija, P. and Kumar, G. (2009). GCSE physical education and the embodiment of gender. *Sport, Education and Society 14*, 383–339. DOI: 10.1080/13573320903217083

Vertinsky, P.A. (1992). Reclaiming space, revisioning the body: The quest for gender-sensitive physical education. *Quest, 44*, 373–396. DOI: 10.1080/00336297.1992.10484063

Weedon, C. (1997). *Feminist practice & poststructuralist theory* (2nd ed.). Malden, MA: Blackwell.

Weiler, K. (1988). *Women teaching for change: Gender, class and power.* South Hadley, MA: Bergin & Garvey.

Weis, L. and Fine, M. (2004). *Working method: Research and social justice.* New York, NY: Routledge.

Whitehead, M. (1990). Meaningful existence, embodiment and physical education. *Journal of Philosophy of Education, 24*, 3–14. DOI: 10.1111/j.1467-9752.1990.tb00219.x

Whitehead, M. (2010). *Physical literacy: Throughout the lifecourse.* London, UK: Routledge.

Wolf, N. (1991). *The beauty myth: How images of beauty are used against women.* New York, NY: William Morrow and Company, Inc.

Wright, J. (1995). A feminist poststructuralist methodology for the study of gender construction in physical education: Description of a study. *Journal of Teaching in Physical Education, 15*, 1–24.

Wright, J. (2000). Bodies, meanings and movement: A comparison of the language of a physical education lesson and a Feldenkrais movement class. *Sport, Education and Society, 5*, 35–49. DOI: 10.1080/135733200114424

Wright, J. and King, R.C. (1990). "I say what I mean", said Alice: An analysis of gendered discourse in physical education. *Journal of Teaching in Physical Education, 10*, 210–225.

Young, I.M. (1980). "Throwing like a girl": a phenomenology of feminine body comportment, motility and spatiality. *Human Studies*, *3*, 137–156. DOI: 10.1007/BF02331805

Chapter 5

Inquiry-based education centred *in* action

> People are naturally curious. They are born learners. Education can either develop or stifle their inclination to ask why and to learn... *Not* encouraging students to question knowledge, society or experience tacitly endorses and supports the status quo. A curriculum that does not challenge the standard syllabus and conditions in society informs students that knowledge and the world are fixed and are fine the way they are, with no role for students to play in transforming them, and no need for change.
>
> Shor, 1992, p. 12

Introduction

Inquiry-based education centred in action is a third critical element in working with girls from an activist approach. Activist research in physical education demonstrates that when teachers use inquiry-based learning centred *in* action, they can and do facilitate girls' active and willing engagement in physical education (Ennis, 1999; Enright and O'Sullivan, 2010a; 2012a; 2012b; Fisette, 2011b; 2011a; 2010; Fisette and Walton, 2014; Oliver, Hamzeh, and McCaughtry, 2009; Oliver and Hamzeh, 2010; Oliver and Lalik, 2004; Oliver, 2010; Oliver and Oesterreich et al., 2015). These scholars have systematically responded to the calls from physical education researchers for teachers to use critical inquiry and critical pedagogy as a means of assisting young people in the process of becoming critical consumers of physical culture (for example, Fitzgerald and Jobling, 2004; Glasby and Macdonald, 2004). They have coupled their responses with the calls from critical and feminist activist scholars to move beyond studying "that which is" and begin to systematically study, "that which might be", and thus have worked within social change projects (Fine, 2007; Freire, 1997; Oliver and Lalik, 2000). Finally, they have responded to larger calls in education for teachers to use inquiry-based learning as a means of social transformation towards interests of equity and justice (O'Connor, Jeanes and Alfrey, 2014; Freire, 1974; 1985; Giroux, 1997; Luke and Gore, 1992; Shannon, 1992; Weiler, 1988; Shor, 1992).

In this chapter we chronicle the advocacy in physical education research for using critical inquiry or critical pedagogies (Devis-Devis, 2006; Wright, Macdonald and Burrows, 2004). We then show how activist scholars have gone beyond advocacy (O'Sullivan, Siedentop and Locke, 1992) to study what happens when we engage girls in inquiry-based projects centred *in* action with the underlying intent to assist girls in the process of naming, critiquing, negotiating and transforming barriers to their learning to value the physically active life.

Critical inquiry/Critical pedagogy in physical education research

As with concepts of student-centredness and embodiment, we see similar inconsistencies in conceptualization around critical inquiry and pedagogy. In his chapter in the *Handbook of Physical Education*, Devis-Devis (2006) argued that alternative and broadly "critical" forms of physical education were present in the literature from the 1970s (for example, Hellison, 1978), though it was not until the late 1980s that a first review paper on socially-critical research in physical education and sport was published (Bain, 1989). One of the earliest uses of the term "critical pedagogy" appeared in Kirk's (1986a) advocacy paper for an inquiry-oriented approach to teacher education, and was later applied to school physical education (Kirk, 1988). According to Kirk (1986a), an inquiry-oriented approach had its roots in action research and critical social and curriculum theory. "New Directions" sociology of education (Young, 1971) had advanced the notion that if the curriculum was socially constructed then teachers themselves could play a part in this process, starting with and rendering problematic the everyday practices of the classroom (Apple, 1979). Evans and Davies first introduced the "new directions" sociology of education into the physical education literature in Evans'

1986 edited collection (Evans 1986). Although Devis-Devis (2006) considered a number of the studies in Evans and Davies book to be underpinned by socially-critical perspectives on physical education, none at the time explicitly used the terms critical pedagogy or inquiry-based education. Moreover, as socially-critical inspired publications appeared in growing numbers through the 1990s, much of this work remained at the level of advocacy, and did not address the challenge implicit in "new directions" sociology that teachers might play an intentional role in the social construction of the curriculum.

O'Sullivan, Siedentop and Locke (1992) were highly critical of this emerging socially-critical discourse in physical education research. They wrote:

> Although the radical literature is long on criticisms of existing practice in physical education, it is short on descriptions of what a radical physical education would look like. What are the goals for physical education derived from a critical-theory perspective? What pedagogical practices are consistent with such goals for physical education and teacher education programmes? What evidence is there that such practices are indeed enlightening and liberating? (p. 225)

Despite their criticism, socially-critical perspectives had arguably become a new orthodoxy in physical education by the time of the publication of the edited collection by Wright, Macdonald and Burrows (2004). This edited volume illustrates the inconsistencies of conceptual clarity surrounding socially-critical approaches to physical education as evidenced in the inclusion of critical inquiry and problem-solving. As Wright's introductory chapter noted, problem-solving referred to specific skills of reasoning whereas critical inquiry referred to examining and challenging the status quo and dominant power relations. Nevertheless, the chapters by Glasby and Macdonald, and Fitzgerald and Jobling, provide evidence of a more action-oriented approach to critical inquiry compared with the initial advocacy papers of the late 1980s and 1990s. At the same time, these studies fall short of the challenges posed by O'Sullivan, Siedentop and Locke (1992) in terms of providing goals, programmes and evidence to support socially-critical approaches.

More recently, the ongoing advocacy for forms of critical inquiry in physical education and related topics (such as health) have resulted in their adoption by writers of state-mandated curricula in New Zealand (Bowes and Bruce, 2011) and Australia (Penney, 2010). Two projects from the Australian States of Queensland and Victoria suggest that progress has been made in meeting the challenge of inquiry-based education to move from advocacy to action. For example, McCuaig et al. (2012) developed a school-based intervention in Queensland focused on health literacy for 13–14 year old students as part of their regular Health and Physical Education programme. This project (see McCuaig, Carroll and Macdonald, 2014) clearly incorporated aspects on inquiry-based learning such as "the construction and critique of 'real-life' scenarios, group decision-making, critical evaluation of e-health resources and website design" (p. 20). Quoting McInerney and McInerney, McCuaig et al. (2012) found that there is a "shift in focus from what the teacher may do to influence learning to what the learner does as an active agent in the learning process" (p. 49). At the same time, the process was initiated through collaboration between university researchers and teachers, and the nature of the learning task determined in advance of consultation with students. The authors note that responsibility for curriculum development and implementation in Queensland rests with the teacher, informed by state mandated curricula. However, there is some evidence to suggest that the incorporation of some elements of inquiry-based learning had the potential to disrupt teacher- student power relations, a feature of student-centred pedagogy we noted in Chapter 3. The report's authors claim only modest outcomes for this intervention. Although teachers and students alike demonstrated a better understanding of aspects of healthy living for adolescents, both showed little insight into the broader socio-cultural and economic determinants of health.

Also in Australia, O'Connor and Alfrey (2013) worked with teachers in two primary schools in Victoria to develop an Active School Travel (AST) unit that involved students in a process of what they named Socio-Ecological Action Research (SEAR), a form of inquiry-based learning. Positioned as "active researchers", the students worked through the processes of defining the issues, planning for action, generating action, and reflecting on the outcomes of the process. O'Connor and Alfrey (2013) noted that although students were positioned as co-researchers, the topic for study was not derived from the students' interests.

We conclude this section with some cautious optimism. Researchers, teachers and state-sponsored curriculum writers are starting to create health-related physical education programmes informed by socially-critical perspectives. At the same time, Leahy, O'Flynn and Wright (2013) claim that there are various and sometimes disparate notions of "the critical" at work in these curriculum reforms. For example, some of these notions of the critical are informed by social justice ideals while others are informed by notions of critical thinking as problem-solving (Wright, 2004). There is a constant danger that notions of the critical are shaped by the discourses of neoliberal ideology. Moreover, these discourses increasingly construct and constitute the idea of education itself (Giroux, 2011; Macdonald, 2003). Since the first appearance of notions such as critical pedagogy and inquiry-oriented approaches in the physical education literature in the 1980s we have seen a proliferation of terminology that Leahy and colleagues claim brings with them specific, and sometimes quite different, visions of and goals for physical education.

Inquiry-based education centred *in* action: an activist approach

> It's the first time I've seen any purpose to PE. Sad but true ... it's not nothing like before... It's more about trying to help us be smart active and confident to use stuff like gyms around where we live. Basically it's helping us be active more than once a week in class, we're helping ourselves be active actually, and PE [used not to] do that and it's also more about us and our lives, and that's first, but that's just not the case for PE that's in most school stuff.
>
> quoted in Enright and O'Sullivan, 2012a, pp. 259–260

Collectively, the activist research studies show that inquiry-based education centred in action facilitates girls' engagement and interest in physical education (for example, Enright and O'Sullivan, 2012a; Fisette and Walton, 2014; Oliver and Hamzeh, 2010). To focus our discussion on inquiry-based education centred in action as a third critical element, we draw on Cochran-Smith and Lytle's notion of inquiry-based learning (1999; 2009). Levy et al. (2013) characterize Cochran-Smith and Lytle's (1999; 2009) work as a powerful conception of inquiry-based learning in that they:

> characterize inquiry as content, outcome, pedagogy, and stance. They contend that if inquiry as content involves the collaborative construction of knowledge, then inquiry as outcome is when teachers and students develop a questioning and critical perspective on educational problems and issues. They further explain that inquiry based pedagogy generates and investigates questions, and inquiry as stance is a grounded theory of action that positions the role of the practitioners and practitioner knowledge as central to the goal of transforming, teaching, learning, leading and school (p. 389).

Cochran-Smith and Lytle's (1999; 2009) notion of inquiry-based learning helps us understand why activist scholars in physical education have relied so heavily on engaging girls in inquiry as part of their research. Inquiry itself challenges the status quo of physical education because it requires us to "fundamentally question how schooling is done" (Short and Burke, 1996, p. 103). These scholars come to their work with the intent not only to identify, but also to work towards changing inequitable environments and practices that impact girls' engagement in physical education. In doing so, they have learned a great deal about how engaging girls in the process of naming, critiquing, negotiating or transforming barriers to their learning, enjoyment, and engagement in physical activity and physical education brings relevancy for girls (for example, Fisette and Walton, 2014; Enright and O'Sullivan, 2010a; Oliver, Hamzeh and McCaughtry, 2009).

It is within this critical element that student-centred pedagogy and critical study of embodiment merge to form a basis from which inquiry-oriented approaches to learning create spaces for teachers and students to take action directed at improving physical activity opportunities for girls. To illustrate this point we will draw on two examples. The first was a project Fisette and her colleague Walton undertook with 9th grade high school girls (Fisette and Walton, 2014) The intent of Fisette and Walton's activist research project was two-fold. Phase one was designed for girls to explore, through inquiry, their sense of self and their embodied identities within a physical education context. Here, they engaged in a variety of inquiry-based tasks designed in part to understand how the girls consumed media and how these media shaped their embodied experiences. The girls kept media logs documenting the "specific programmes, websites, social media and networks, and the amount of time they utilized the form of media" (p. 9). This inquiry-based task was the inspiration for phase two of the research.

Phase two was action-oriented and inspired by what the girls were learning about how media texts influenced their embodied sense of self. The girls claimed that music and television allowed them to escape from reality as well as provide a space that influenced their behaviour and perspectives. In particular they noted that the show "If you Really Knew Me" inspired them to not jump to conclusions about people until they had the opportunity to understand their life situation. The girls articulated that within their physical education class one of the barriers to students' engagement and enjoyment was a lack of communication and trust and that this caused animosity among many of the students. They were keenly aware of the bullying that was taking place in physical education class and wanted to do something to stop it.

The girls wanted to conduct a version of the reality show "If you Really Knew Me" in their class as a way to stop the bullying so that students would feel more comfortable in physical education. Responding to the girls' interests, Fisette and Walton (2014) helped them to create a survey that would allow them to understand each other better. Many of the questions addressed issues related to embodiment. For example, they asked: "Have you ever been judged or treated differently because of your skin color?" "Is there someone in your life who consistently puts you down?" "Have you ever suffered from body issues or low self-esteem?" They also asked: "If people really knew you, what would you want them to know?" (p. 144). Rather than surveying only their physical education class, they decided to survey the entire school population, approximately 1,300 students. From the surveys they analyzed the data and created a video that was aired in all homeroom classes. One of the unintended outcomes of this project was what it did for the girls' sense of empowerment. Fisette and Walton (2014) write

> They were overjoyed that they were the first students, according to the physical education teachers, that ever surveyed the entire school population, let alone create a video that was aired throughout the school. Individually, and as a group, they articulated that they felt empowered for having the opportunity to take action on an issue that was important to them... [Mia, one of the girls wrote], 'It made me think more about what others go through and I enjoyed putting my time in to make a

difference. It made me more open-minded. It made me realize that I am more judgmental than I thought. I would really like people to realize how much goes on in others' lives. I feel that what we have done could really help others' (p. 147).

This example illuminates how opportunities to critically inquire into issues of embodiment, coupled with student-centred pedagogy, created the space for the teachers and students to work together to take action directed at making physical education better for students. As Short and Burke (1996) remind us, curriculum as inquiry changes relationships between students and teachers as well as how we view knowledge and who has that knowledge. This example illustrates Cochran-Smith and Lytle's (1999; 2009) notion of inquiry-based learning as content, outcome, pedagogy, and stance.

Although Fisette and Walton's example illuminates how the girls' interests were in taking action directed at creating the conditions that would foster a class environment where students respected rather than bullied one another, this next example illustrates girls' interests in negotiating a physical activity curricula. Working in an Irish context in a three-year long participatory action research project Enright and O'Sullivan (2010a; 2010b; 2012a; 2012b, 2013) discuss the importance of negotiating the curriculum with girls. Their work is based on the ideas that students are primary stakeholders in their physical education experiences and should be recognized as co-constructors of knowledge and of action. They quote Australian curriculum expert, Garth Boomer, who wrote in 1992, "Negotiating the curriculum means deliberately planning to invite students to contribute to, and to modify, the educational programme, so that they will have a real investment both in the learning journey and it the outcomes" (in Enright and O'Sullivan 2010a, p. 204).

For the girls in Enright and O'Sullivan's (2010a) project, negotiating the curriculum involved "naming inequities; broadening horizons; and change agency" (p. 208). Utilizing participatory action research methodologies as pedagogical tasks with which to engage girls in inquiry (Enright and O'Sullivan, 2010b), they started with a six-week phase designed to assist the girls to name physical education inequities. Here, they worked to get to know the girls, what they valued and found interesting, and what they experienced as barriers to their physical education enjoyment and engagement by having the girls create task books. These books included a personal biography, a physical activity timeline and profile, and reflections on the girls' perceptions of physical education and alternative possibilities. What Enright learned in this phase was that the girls disengaged from physical education because the curriculum did not reflect their voices in any way, did not provide girls with choices of activities, and was viewed by the girls as "stupid PE" (p. 209).

Given where the girls were starting, unsure of what forms of physical activity were available to them, the next phase was designed to broaden the girls' horizons of possible physical education curricula. Drawing on the work of Maxine Greene, Enright hoped to assist the girls to imagine alternatives to their current physical education programme. To do so she engaged the girls in a variety of "taster sessions" over a 10-week period. In these sessions the girls would try different forms of content taught by Enright. A debriefing section where the girls evaluated their experiences of the content in relation to their learning, interest, and future change followed each taster lesson. Each taster session built on what Enright was learning from the girls through the debriefings. What ultimately happened was that the girls and Enright held a "curriculum decision-making session" (p. 210), where they collectively negotiated aspects of the content as well as pedagogical processes. One of the things the girls wanted as non-negotiable was that "we have to listen to the teachers because they are listening to us" (Enright and O'Sullivan, 2010a, p. 211).

Focusing on girls as change-agents, in the final phase of the research, Enright worked with the girls to "take responsibility for rethinking and changing their PE and physical activity experiences" (Enright and O'Sullivan, 2010a; 2012b). During this phase, the girls collaborated with Enright to co-construct an eight-week curriculum unit grounded in the girls' previous inquiry-based work. Collectively they acted together to design a unit that would assist girls in trying "new things in PE that will help us to like being active and help us to be active more and it will be good fun" (Enright and O'Sullivan, 2010a, p. 212).

Enright's findings revealed that the girls' increased involvement in the curriculum decision-making process impacted their engagement in physical education in four specific ways. These included the girls' increased participation and being prepared (dressed) to participate, an increase in learning and taking responsibility for theirs and other's learning, increased accountability for their roles and responsibilities within the class, and an awareness of physical activity possibilities in their communities coupled with an increase in self-confidence to pursue those possibilities. In these findings, we again hear echoes of Cochran-Smith and Lytle's (1999; 2009) notion of inquiry-based learning as content, outcome, pedagogy and stance.

Clear in Enright's study are the critical elements of student-centred pedagogy, opportunities to study issues of embodiment, and inquiry-based education centred *in* action. The value in using inquiry, *centred in* action, as a way to engage girls in physical education was reflected not only in the girls' actions, but also in their words, "we're more in charge", "it makes you think", "we can change things, make a difference" and "it was just good fun" (Enright and O'Sullivan, 2012a, p. 44). Her example illustrates how a shift in pedagogy created opportunities for girls to find meaning and relevancy in their physical education class, and similar to the girls in Fisette and Walton's (2014) study, they appreciated being valued for what they could do to improve their physical education experience. As one girl wrote:

> We bring our lives into class like with the scrappin' the media stuff we do and talking about how magazines tell us we have to be skinny and eat low fat and diet everything and making us feel bad about ourselves and scrapping the photographs of our lives and communities that we took as well ... it's like in a way we're giving PE a shake, making it mean something.
>
> quoted in Enright and O'Sullivan, 2012a, p. 259

Physical education re-conceptualized

> Curriculum ceases to be a thing, and it is more than a process. It becomes a verb, an action, a social practice, and private meaning, and a public hope. Curriculum is not just the site of our labor, it becomes the product of our labor, changing as we are changed by it.
>
> Pinar et al., 1995, p. 848

According to Oliver and Oesterreich (2013) utilizing inquiry centred in student voice as a guide to understanding what facilitates young people's interest, motivation and learning involves a shift in how we conceptualize physical education. What becomes clear when we look across the activist research with girls in physical education is a theoretical shift in how these scholars begin to think about physical education differently. The Fisette and Walton (2014) and Enright and O'Sullivan (2010a) examples illustrate this shift. Part of what activist researchers have done with girls in their attempts to find ways to better facilitate girls' engagement was to start from where girls were, work to assist girls in naming what facilitated and hindered their interest, motivation, and learning in physical education, and intentionally helped girls negotiate or transform the barriers they identified. Through these processes, physical education curriculum ultimately becomes a verb: "an action, a social practice ... a public hope ... changing as we are changed by it" (Pinar et al., 1995, p. 848).

Inquiry-based education becomes central to a profound shift in thinking about what physical education *is* and *might be*. When we think about physical education through inquiry-based approaches to learning that are centred *in* action – action that directly enhances the quality of girls' physical education experiences – we can no longer look at curriculum as fixed. That is, the contents of physical activity and sport can no longer be what Metzler (2005) calls the "organizing centre" for programmes. Rather, physical education becomes a process of inquiry-oriented tasks involving particular forms of learning, teaching and curriculum designed to ultimately improve current physical activity environments and practices in ways that better facilitate girls' engagement, learning, and motivation for valuing the physically active life. Short and Burke (1996) remind us, "inquiry involves a major shift in thinking... Inquiry is theoretically based on collaborative relationships, not the hierarchies or control common in most schools" (p. 35).

For girls to learn to value the physically active life requires that they learn how to name, critique, negotiate or transform barriers they identify as being problematic to *their* motivation, enjoyment, engagement and learning. This in turn shifts the focus from the teacher as the primary source of knowledge to the teachers and the students working in collaboration to identify specific curricular needs (Shor, 1992; Short and Burke, 1996; O'Connor, Jeanes and Alfrey, 2014). In Enright's study, she worked with the girls to co-create an eight-week unit whereby the girls got to "try new things in PE that will help us to like being active". Inquiry thus becomes the means by which students and teachers engage with one another. Inquiry becomes the means by which students and teachers base their decisions and their negotiations. Inquiry becomes the central pedagogical process for developing, implementing and assessing physical education curricula. A shift from content as the organizing centre to inquiry-based pedagogy as the organizing centre ultimately requires a reconceptualization of physical education.

Re-conceptualizing physical education: implications

In his comparison of "traditional" and "progressive" education that lies at the heart of *Experience and Education*, Dewey (1938) wrote that:

> It is, accordingly, a much more difficult task to work out the kinds of materials, of methods, and of social relationships that are appropriate to the new education than is the case with traditional education. I think many of the difficulties experienced in the conduct of progressive schools and many of the criticisms levelled against them arise from this source (p. 29).

For Dewey, the challenge for what he called "progressive" education was to develop school curricula that were based in the everyday experiences of students rather than on an accumulated and largely unquestioned "great cultural heritage". More recently, as we noted earlier in this chapter, O'Sullivan, Siedentop and Locke (1992) commented that "the radical agenda" of socially-critical approaches "will demand dramatic programme revisions and powerful new instructional procedures" (p. 227), as developments at the curricular level will be essential for the implementation of any new vision for physical education.

Building on student-centred pedagogy and pedagogies of embodiment, we have argued that inquiry-based education centred in action brings about a shift in the organizing centre for physical education away from curriculum content alone towards the interacting and interdependent dimensions of pedagogy that are learning, teaching and curriculum. This shift requires a reconceptualization of physical education in which the traditional reliance, for example, on the cultural heritage of games and sports is no longer sufficient. But if physical education is to be shaped for inquiry-based education centred in the actions of students in collaboration with their teachers, what are the implications at the programme level? What issues arise for activist researchers for what Dewey saw as a "much more difficult task" than that required of traditional educators?

In the next chapter we seek to answer these questions implied by the shift in organizing centre for physical education by elaborating one way in which these three critical elements of activist work can be implemented. Prior to entering into this discussion, we want to close this chapter by posing and seeking to respond to two questions that our reading of the literature of "traditional versus progressive" education invariably raises. The first is if we no longer rely on the "grand cultural heritage" to organize the curriculum, and we organize programmes instead through inquiry-oriented tasks in the experiences of students, does this mean "anything goes"? A second question that often follows is that if student inquiry is the basis of programmes, what about excellence and depth of learning?

A response to the first question regarding "anything goes" was in part provided in Chapter 3 where we noted that attending to students' voices does not always mean doing whatever students want. Moreover, in proposing valuing the physically active life as the main theme of this approach to physical education, we suggest that the range of possible options for programme development is immediately identified. Clearly, this theme suggests that physical activity remains a medium for learning in physical education, but not the only one. As we argued in Chapter 4, although the experience of physical activity is fundamental to a pedagogy of embodiment, it is equally important to create opportunities for girls to critically study issues that influence how they are learning to think and feel about their bodies.

If the experience of physical activity is to remain a medium for learning in physical education, then the second question about excellence and depth of learning comes in to sharper focus. Dewey (1938) argued that the principle of continuity of experience is the aspect of "progressive" education so often missing at the point of implementation of programmes. Nevertheless, for Dewey, the criterion of continuity was the basis for identifying educative experiences. He emphasized the importance of the collaboration of the teacher and the student in facilitating an experience that "arouses curiosity, strengthens initiative, and sets up desires and purposes" (p. 38). Dewey argued that:

> Every experience is a moving force. Its value can only be judged on the ground of what it moves toward and into. The

> greater maturity of experience which should belong to the adult as educator puts him [or her] in a position to evaluate each experience of the young in a way in which the one having the less mature experience cannot do. It is then the business of the educator to see in what direction an experience is heading. (p. 38)

This response to the issue of excellence and depth of learning cannot be framed by the cannon of traditional sports and games, which takes high performance (and typically male professional sports) as its ultimate marker of achievement and thus as the basis for learning in physical education. The Deweyan-inspired response rests on an experiential continuum that provides inquiry-based education centred in action with a direction that each individual learner is guided by "arousing curiosity, strengthening initiative and setting up desires and purposes". The moving force of experience is towards further experiences that broaden and deepen learning on the journey towards valuing the physically active life. In Pinar's terms, curriculum thus becomes a verb, a process, and its experience a hope for the future.

Conclusion

In this chapter we reviewed how socially-critical research has been used and described in the physical education literature, noting a lack of consistency in its conceptualization. We then described a third critical element, inquiry-based education centred in action. Within this critical element, student-centred pedagogy and critical study of embodiment merge to form a basis from which inquiry-oriented approaches to learning create spaces for teachers and students to take action directed at improving physical activity opportunities for girls. In the next chapter we will introduce our final critical element, *Listening and Responding*. Here we will discuss one possible pedagogical approach for embedding in practice opportunities to listen and respond to students over time.

References

Apple, M.W. (1979). *Ideology and Curriculum*. London, UK: Routledge & Kegan Paul.

Bain, L.L. (1989). Interpretive and critical research in sport and physical education. *Research Quarterly for Exercise and Sport, 60*(1), 21–24. DOI: 0.1080/02701367.1989.10607408

Bowes, M. and Bruce, J. (2011). Curriculum liquefaction (shifting sands) in senior school physical education in New Zealand: Critical pedagogical approaches and dilemmas. *Asia-Pacific Journal of Health, Sport and Physical Education*, 2(3–4), 17–33. DOI: 10.1080/18377122.2011.9730357

Cochran-Smith, M. and Lytle, S.L. (1999). Relationships of knowledge and practice: Teacher learning in communities. *Review of Research in Education*, 24, 249–305. DOI:10.3102/0091732X024001249

Cochran-Smith, M. and Lytle, S.L. (2009). *Inquiry as stance: Practitioner research for the next generation.* New York, NY: Teachers College Press.

Devis-Devis, J. (2006) Socially critical research perspectives in physical education, pp. 37–58, in Kirk, D., Macdonald, D. and O'Sullivan, M. (2006, Eds.) *Handbook of Physical Education* London, UK: Sage.

Dewey, J. (1938) *Education and experience.* New York, NY: Macmillan.

Ennis, C.D. (1999). Creating culturally relevant curriculum for disengaged girls. *Sport, Education and Society,* 4, 31–49. DOI: 10.1080/1357332990040103

Enright, E. and O'Sullivan, M. (2010a). "Can I do it in my pyjamas?" Negotiating a physical education curriculum with teenage girls. *European Physical Education Review,* 16, 203–222. DOI: 10.1177/1356336X10382967

Enright, E. and O'Sullivan, M. (2010b). "Carving a new order of experience" with young people in physical education: Participatory action research as a pedagogy of possibility. In M. O'Sullivan and A. MacPhail (Eds.), *Young people's voices in physical education and youth sport,* (pp. 163–185). London, UK: Routledge.

Enright, E. and O'Sullivan M. (2012a). Physical education "In all sorts of corners": Student activists transgressing formal physical education curricular boundaries. *Research Quarterly for Exercise and Sport 83*, 255–267. DOI: 10.1080/02701367.2012.10599856

Enright, E. and O'Sullivan, M. (2012b). Producing different knowledge and producing knowledge differently: Rethinking physical education research and practice through participatory visual methods. *Sport, Education and Society, 17*, 35–55. DOI: 10.1080/13573322.2011.607911

Enright, E, and O'Sullivan, M. (2013). "Now, I'm magazine detective the whole time": Listening and responding to young people's complex experiences of popular physical culture. *Journal of Teaching in Physical Education, 32*, 394–418.

Evans, J. (1986) (Ed) *Physical education, sport and schooling: Studies in the sociology of physical education.* Lewes, UK: Falmer.

Fine, M. (2007). Feminist designs for difference. In S.N. Hesse-Biber, (Ed.),

Handbook of Feminist Research: Theory and Praxis, (pp. 613–620). Thousand Oaks, CA: Sage.

Fisette, J. (2010). Getting to know your students. *Journal of Physical Education and Dance*, *81*(7), 42–49. DOI: 10.1080/07303084.2010.10598508

Fisette, J.L. (2011a). Exploring how girls navigate their embodied identities in physical education. *Physical Education and Sport Pedagogy, 16*, 179–196. DOI: 10.1080/17408989.2010.535199

Fisette, J.L. (2011b). Negotiating power within high school girls' exploratory projects in physical education. *Women in Sport and Physical Activity Journal, 20*, 73–90.

Fisette, J.L. and Walton, T.A. (2014). "If you really knew me" ... I am empowered through action. *Sport, Education and Society,* 131–152. DOI:10.1080/13573322.2011.643297

Fitzgerald, H. and Jobling, A. (2004). Student-centered research: Working with disabled students. In J. Wright, D. Macdonald and L. Burrows (Eds.) *Critical inquiry and problem-solving in physical education* (pp. 74–92) London, UK: Routledge.

Freire, P. (1974). *Pedagogy of the oppressed.* New York, NY: Seabury Press.

Freire, P. (1985). *The politics of education: culture, power, and liberation.* Westport, CT: Bergin & Garvey.

Freire, P. (1997). *Pedagogy of the Oppressed.* Continuum: New York, NY.

Giroux, H.A. (1997). *Pedagogy and the politics of hope: Theory, culture, and schooling.* Boulder, CO: Westview Press.

Giroux, H. (2011) *On Critical Pedagogy.* New York: Continuum.

Glasby, T. and Macdonald, D. (2004). Negotiating the curriculum: Challenging the social relationships in teaching. In J. Wright, D. Macdonald and L. Burrows, (Eds.), *Critical Inquiry and Problem-solving in Physical Education* (pp.133–144). London, UK: Routledge.

Hellison, D. (1978). *Beyond bats and balls: Alienated (and other) youth in the gym.* Washington, DC: AAHPERD.

Kirk, D. (1986). A critical pedagogy for teacher education: Towards an inquiry-oriented approach. *Journal of Teaching in Physical Education, 5*, 230–246.

Kirk, D. (1988). *Physical education and curriculum study: A critical introduction.* London, UK: Croom Helm.

Leahy, D., O'Flynn, G. and Wright, J. (2013). A critical "critical inquiry" proposition in health and physical education. *Asia-Pacific Journal of Health, Sport and Physical Education*, 4, 175–187. DOI: 10.1080/18377122.2013.805479

Levy, B.L.M., Thomas, E.E., Drago, K. and Rex, L.A. (2013). Examining studies of inquiry-based learning in three fields of education: Sparking generative conversation. *Journal of Teacher Education, 64*, 387–408. DOI: 10.1177/0022487113496430

Luke, C. and Gore, J. (1992). *Feminisms and critical pedagogy*. New York, NY: Routledge.

Macdonald, D. (2003). Curriculum change and the post-modern world: Is the school curriculum-reform movement an anachronism? *Journal of Curriculum Studies*, *35*, 139–149. DOI: 10.1080/00220270210157605

McCuaig, L., Carroll, K., Coore, S., Rossi, T., Macdonald, D., Bush, R., Ostini, R. and Hay, P., (2012). *Developing health literacy through school based health education: Can reality match rhetoric?* (Phase I Report). Brisbane: University of Queensland.

McCuaig, L., Carroll, K. and Macdonald, D. (2014). Enacting critical health literacy in the Australian secondary school curriculum: the possibilities posed by e-health. *Asia-Pacific Journal of Health, Sport and Physical Education*, *5*, 217–231. DOI: 10.1080/18377122.2014.940809

Metzler, M.W. (2005). *Instructional models for physical education* (2nd ed.). Scottsdale, AZ: Holcomb Hathaway.

O'Connor, J. and Alfrey, L. (2013). "Activating the curriculum: a socioecological action research frame for health and physical education." *Sport, Education and Society*, 1–19. doi: 10.1080/13573322.2013.789013

O'Connor, J., Jeanes, R. and Alfrey, L. (2014). "Authentic inquiry-based learning in Health and Physical Education: A case study of 'r/evolutionary' practice" *Physical Education and Sport Pedagogy*.

O'Sullivan, M. and MacPhail, A. (Eds.). (2010). *Young People's Voices in Physical Education and Youth Sport*. London, UK: Routledge.

O'Sullivan, M., Siedentop, D. and Locke, L.L. (1992). Toward collegiality: Competing viewpoints among teacher educators. *Quest*, 44(2), 266–280. DOI: 10.1080/00336297.1992.10484054

Oliver, K.L. (2010). The body, physical activity and inequity: Learning to listen *with* girls *through* action. In M. O'Sullivan and A. MacPhail (Eds.), *Young people's voices in physical education and youth sport* (pp. 31–48). London, UK: Routledge.

Oliver, K.L. and Hamzeh, M. (2010). "The boys won't let us play": 5th grade *Mestizas* publicly challenge physical activity discourse at school. *Research Quarterly for Exercise and Sport, 81*, 39–51. DOI: 10.1080/02701367.2010.10599626

Oliver, K.L., Hamzeh, M. and McCaughtry, N. (2009). "Girly girls *can* play games/*las niñas pueden jugar tambien*": Co-creating a curriculum of possibilities with 5th grade girls. *Journal of Teaching in Physical Education, 28*, 90–110.

Oliver, K.L. and Lalik, R. (2000). *Bodily knowledge: Learning about equity and justice with adolescent girls*. New York, NY: Peter Lang Publishing, Inc.

Oliver, K.L. and Lalik, R. (2004). Critical inquiry on the body in girls' physical education classes: A critical poststructural analysis. *Journal of Teaching in Physical Education 23*, 162–195.

Oliver, K.L. and Oesterreich, H.A. (2013). Student-centred inquiry as curriculum as a model for field-based teacher education. *Journal of Curriculum Studies, 45*, 394–417.

Oliver, K.L. and Oesterreich, H.A. *with* R. Aranda, J. Archuleta, C. Blazer, K. De La Cruz, D. Martinez, J. McConnell, M. Osta, L. Parks and R. Robinson. (2015). "The sweetness of struggle": Innovation in PETE through student-centred inquiry *as* curriculum in a physical education methods course. *Physical Education and Sport Pedagogy 20*(1), 97–115. DOI: 10.1080/17408989.2013.803527

Penney, D. (2010) Health and Physical Education in Australia: A defining time? *Asia-Pacific Journal of Health, Sport and Physical Education*, 1(1), 5–10.

Pinar, W.F., Reynolds, W.H., Slattery, P. and Taubman, P.M (1995). *Understanding Curriculum*. New York, NY: Peter Lang Publishing.

Shannon, P. (1992). *Becoming political: Readings and writings in the politics of literacy education*. Portsmouth, NH: Heinemann.

Shor, I. (1992). *Empowering education: Critical teaching for social change*. Chicago, IL: University of Chicago Press.

Short, K.G. and Burke, C. (1996). Examining our beliefs and practices through inquiry. *Language Arts, 73*(2), 97–104.

Weiler, K. (1988). *Women teaching for change: Gender, class and power*. South Hadley, MA: Bergin & Garvey.

Wright, J. (2004). Critical inquiry and problem-solving in physical education. In Wright, J., Macdonald, D., and Burrows, L. (Eds.). (2004). *Critical inquiry and problem solving in physical education*. London, UK: Falmer.

Wright, J., Macdonald, D. and Burrows, L. (Eds.). (2004). *Critical inquiry and problem solving in physical education*. London, UK: Falmer.

Young, M.F.D. (Ed.). (1971). *Knowledge and Control: New directions for the sociology of education*. London, UK: Collier-Macmillan.

Chapter 6

Listening and Responding Over Time

With Heather A. Oesterreich

Introduction

> Like if we come here on Tuesday, on Thursday you come back and you, and you, we can tell that you thought about what we said... Because, I mean, you have somethin' to say about it, and then you also go back to, you know, like what we said earlier. *Nicole*
>
> Oliver and Lalik, 2000, p. 108

"It takes impatience with the way things are to motivate people to make changes, but then it takes patience to study and to develop the projects through which constructive learning and change are made" (Shor, 1992, p. 25). Impatient with the inadequacies of physical education for girls, in 1996, I (Kim) started on what would become a patient and systematic inquiry into how to better facilitate girls' engagement in physical education and physical activity in ways that were relevant and meaningful to them. This chapter is different from the first three critical elements insofar as much more of its content is derived from my line of inquiry spanning eighteen years of working to support girls' physical activity and physical education engagement and enjoyment. Although the issue of time does cut across all activist research in the same ways with which the other three critical elements do, we will write differently in this chapter.

The final critical element for engaging girls in physical education is a teacher's willingness to listen and respond to girls over time. There are three themes centred in time that are consistent across the body of activist research in physical education with girls. The first is that it takes time on the part of the teacher to help girls find ways to communicate what they know and how they feel in a language that allows them to begin to name how things might be better in physical education. Second, it takes time to develop the types of relationships where girls are willing to tell teachers or researchers what they think and how they feel. Third, it takes time to figure out in collaboration with girls how to negotiate their self-identified barriers to physical education and physical activity enjoyment and engagement.

We want to be clear about what we are claiming here as activist research and why this chapter of necessity takes a different form from the previous three in so far as there is no overview of related literature in physical education research. We acknowledge that physical education researchers inspired and informed by anthropological and interpretative research paradigms have conducted fieldwork in physical education settings that require lengthy periods of time in the field. This research, conducted over a thirty-year period includes, for example, ethnographic studies of co-educational classes and gender (Evans et al., 1987; Griffin, 1984), teachers and curriculum innovation (Kirk, 1986; Sparkes, 1986), gender and girls' physical education (Scraton, 1992), gender and initial teacher education (Flintoff, 1993), teaching and learning TGfU (Brooker et al., 2000), teachers' pedagogical content knowledge (Rovegno et al., 2001), young people and disability (Fitzgerald, 2005), boys and masculinities (Tischler and McCaughtry, 2011), and teaching in urban schools (Fitzpatrick, 2013). Similarities between this line of research and activist research is that time in the field allows researchers to gain a depth of understanding and a grasp of the nuances of local cultures that "the tourist never sees" (Locke, 1974). What marks the activist research as different from this other research in physical education is that time in the field is primarily for pedagogical purposes. It is concerned first and foremost with making a difference and thus shaping what is possible in physical education for and with girls.

Listening and responding to girls over time is imperative given the consistent findings from activist research in physical education that illuminates the challenge in helping girls put language to experience (for example, Oliver, Hamzeh and McCaughtry, 2009; Enright and O'Sullivan, 2010). Although some reasons for girls' disengagement from physical education are reported across many types of research, the issues are more complex and are often at a pre-conscious level for girls, as we discussed in Chapter 4. Activist scholars have needed to work across time and in creative ways to help girls name the meanings of their experiences in ways that allow both girls and researchers to use these experiences as a springboard for understanding, critique, and ultimately change. Listening and responding across time in part facilitates a teacher's ability to continually seek girls' knowledge that can grow and become more focused and sophisticated as meanings around enjoyment and engagement in physical education or physical activity continue to be articulated.

The second theme that activist researchers in physical education have consistently reported, is that it takes time to develop the types of relationships where girls *are* willing to tell teachers or researchers what they think and how they feel. Kids have learned over their years in school that many teachers don't want to know what students think, they want to hear particular answers. As girls get older they learn these teacher-pleasing responses that are not only sought, but are also expected (Enright and O'Sullivan, 2012b). In her three-year activist research study, Enright's participants, like many of Oliver's (for example, 1999; 2009), offered responses in the beginning of the studies that the girls thought the researchers wanted to hear. For example, the girls Enright was working with were over-estimating in their journals the amount of physical activity they were doing after school. It wasn't until later in the study that the girls reported they were not being accurate because they thought she wanted to hear something specific. They were not unlike the girls in Oliver's (1999) study who early on were willing to talk about how fashion influenced how they were experiencing their bodies, but were not willing to talk about how race and racism were pivotal to how they were learning to experience their bodies until the study was almost over. Or, the girls in Oliver, Hamzeh and McCaughtry's (2009) study who, early on, claimed that their main barriers to physical activity engagement were a result of them being a "girly girl". It wasn't until later that they started to discuss that what prevented them from being active were the types of activity choices offered in physical education, their fear of being hurt, and their dislike of how the boys were treating them. These issues took longer to uncover because the girls worried about what might happen if they offered information that ultimately would challenge a teacher's practice.

Neither Enright nor Oliver would have gone beyond the "teacher-pleasing" responses if their studies were short term, or if the researchers were not continually seeking to respond pedagogically to what the girls were telling them. To be able to really work with girls, girls would have to trust that the adults are genuine in their intentions; this is why listening and responding across time is pivotal. As Enright and O'Sullivan (2012a) show: "Teachers need to be willing to invest this time, because developing meaningful collaborative relationships with students will take longer than telling students what to do" (p. 263). We need to keep this advice at the forefront when we work to listen and respond to our students. Teachers, for example, cannot assume they understand students if they only ask them for their input at the beginning of the school year. We will not get to where we can see the micro level impact of our pedagogy (Gee, 2000), unless we build into our practice systematic and continual ways of seeking student input, then respond pedagogically to what we are hearing and learning from our students (Oliver and Oesterreich, 2013).

The third theme with respect to time that cuts across all activist research with girls in physical education, is that it takes time to figure out how to negotiate girls' self-identified barriers to their physical activity engagement and enjoyment. Sometimes teachers have to try things to see what does and does not work. This is where student-centred pedagogy and inquiry-based education centred in action become so useful. Short and Burke (1996) note that: "The classroom contexts and social relationships that most powerfully support inquiry are those based in education for democracy (Edelsky, 1994). Inquiry is theoretically based on collaborative relationships, not the hierarchies of control common in most schools" (p. 35). Thus, teachers, with students, inquire into what needs to happen to make physical education relevant and meaningful, then try to work in ways that create change. Sometimes this change is good, other times teachers need to keep working with students and looking to find better ways to facilitate change. Take, for example, the girls in Enright's study. Despite the changes that they were making to their physical education programme, what became clear over time was that these were not doing anything to facilitate girls' participation in physical activity outside of school, a goal that they had sought within their physical education class. It was at this point Enright realized that if she were to respond to what she was learning from the girls, she would need to shift the focus of her research. Because she wanted to be responsive to the girls with whom she worked, she sought funding to support an after school activity club for the girls so that they might have more opportunities to engage in physical activity.

Unless a teacher is committed to listening and responding across time, change is not always possible. In the next section we will describe one way teachers can listen and respond to their students over time (Oliver and Oesterreich, 2013; Oliver and Oesterreich et al., 2015). This approach to listening and responding to students over time was derived from the collective learning of eighteen years of research that, at the centre, was about listening and responding to girls in order to better facilitate their enjoyment and engagement in physical activity and physical education (for example, Oliver, 1999, 2001; Oliver and Lalik, 2000; 2004; Oliver, Hamzeh and McCaughtry, 2009; Oliver and Hamzeh, 2010; Oliver and Oesterreich, 2013; 2015). The next section, unlike the other parts of this book, is written from the "I" more often than the "we". We also write the inclusive "student" rather than "girls" because the approach to listening and responding that we will describe is based on research Oliver and Oesterreich have been doing in co-educational classrooms. This approach to listening and responding is one way to merge student-centred pedagogy, inquiry-based education centred in action, and critical study of embodiment in class contexts where girls and boys are together.

Student-centred inquiry *as* curriculum: a systematic way of listening and responding

> If knowledge is constitutive of the world then our choices about what to teach, how to teach, and how to interpret the texts we teach are ethical choices. They are choices about the sort of world we want to live in. They are choices about what sort of life that world will support. They are choices about a consciousness that projects the world.
>
> Pagano, 1993, p. xv

Seeking to understand girls from their perspectives when I (Kim) began my work in 1996, I was intentional in the types of methods I used to elicit and support girls' views. Working first with a critical literacy scholar Rosary Lalik, I worked to support the girls' voices through tasks I invited them to complete. Weekly, we planned ways to communicate respectful listening while at the same time strove to help the girls elaborate their experiences, critique their practices, and imagine and enact alternative and more equitable possibilities for their lives (Oliver and Lalik, 2000). This process has been the basis for eighteen years of activist research with girls. Although the tasks that I have used to understand girls' experiences, nurture girls' abilities to think critically, and support girls' desires for more equitable change have at times been very different, what has remained constant is my intentional attempt at listening and responding to what I was hearing and not hearing pedagogically.

In 2009, twelve years into my academic career, having had some very successful engagements with supporting girls as they learned to identify, critique, and seek to make changes that would better facilitate their enjoyment or engagement in physical education and physical activity, I decided it was time to figure out how to work with pre-service teachers in the ways I worked to listen and respond to girls. I was no longer satisfied with what I was starting to see as an incommensurability between how I worked with girls in a research setting and how I prepared pre-service teachers to work with youth. I knew that if real change in physical education programmes were to exist in my field, then I would need to fundamentally change how we were doing teacher education. I needed to find a way to model for my students how to work with youth in ways that were student-centred and inquiry-based.

Teaching pre-service teachers to utilize inquiry centred in student voice as a guide for understanding what facilitates and hinders young people's interests, motivation, and learning as we would come to learn, would involve a theoretical shift in how we conceptualized curriculum for teacher education and secondary schools (Oliver and Oesterreich, 2013). I began this shift in 2009, when I decided to study the process of preparing pre-service teachers to learn to utilize student voice and inquiry-based forms of learning in my teacher education courses. I decided to redesign my secondary methods course to be school–based, whereby 90 per cent of the course took place in a local high school where my pre-service teachers and I worked with 25 high school students enrolled in the required freshman-level physical education course. As part of the design, I planned the course so I could model for my pre-service teachers an approach for working with youth. The course experiences were aimed at helping the pre-service teachers learn how to do student-centred and inquiry-based teaching with high school students in order to identify barriers to adolescents' physical activity, critically examine these barriers, and work with the youth to imagine and implement alternative types of activity possibilities.

Knowing that I would need an outside collaborator if I were to study my own practice, I began working with my colleague Heather Oesterreich. At the time, she was the director of secondary education at the institution where I taught and had a long history of doing research with marginalized youth in schools and prisons. Her work was aimed at understanding how to challenge and change the status quo of K-12 schools that fail to meet the needs of many of our students (Camp and Oesterreich, 2010; Oesterreich, 2007; Oesterreich and Flores, 2009). Together, we analyzed the data collected during the semester-long methods course. These data included three 2-hour interviews with each of the pre-service teachers (done by Heather), all student-generated course work, field observations, and debriefing meetings. What we eventually termed "Student-Centred Inquiry *as* Curriculum", which we will describe next, is the result of analyzing how I was working with pre-service teachers and how I was requiring them to simultaneously work with youth. This approach is one systematic possibility for listening and responding to students over time. In the next part of the chapter we will describe each aspect of "student-centred inquiry *as* curriculum" then offer one example of what it looks like in practice with youth.

Building the Foundation. The foundation of student-centred inquiry *as* curriculum is to co-create an environment that allows for mutual understanding, respect, and learning among all participants involved in the educational setting. We need to create valued spaces where students can speak, and where we as teachers re-tune our ears so that we can hear what they are saying and redirect our actions in response to what we hear (Cook-Sather 2009, 2006, Schultz 2003). The foundation was designed to help the pre-service teachers understand the needs and interests of high school students with respect to physical activity, physical education, and the importance of a safe learning environment, help the high school students feel valued for their knowledge and perceptions of their worlds, and help the teacher educator better understand the pre-service teachers' beliefs about youth and physical activity.

Planning. Planning requires simultaneously matching young people's interests, motivation, and learning with teachers' knowledge of their content. Every time the pre-service teachers develop lesson plans, they need to identify how their lessons relate

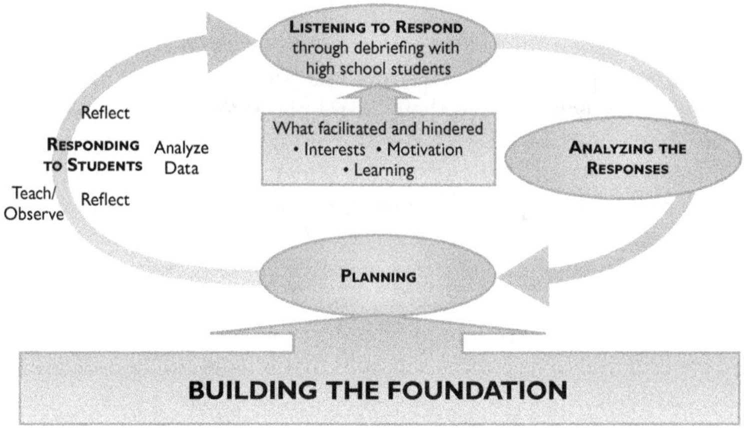

Figure 6.1 Diagram of Student-Centred Inquiry *as* Curriculum

to student voice. The content of the lessons must be connected to the state standards in some capacity, but not reflect predesigned traditional curriculum.

Responding to Students. Responding to students allows the pre-service teachers to learn about teaching from the perspective of a teacher and an outside observer. In this process, students either teach or they observe and collect data. As the teacher they teach, reflect on their teaching, receive observational data from their peers and analyze it, and reflect on their data analysis. In the role of observer, the pre-service teachers collect data on different aspects of the class such as peer interactions, teacher behaviours (feedback, interactions), and body language of students. The observations centre on factors that influence young people's interests, motivation, and learning of the content. For teachers, this phase could repeat itself based on one content area strand.

Listening to Respond. In this phase, high school students are debriefed. The purpose of this is two-fold. First, it creates a space for high school students to reflect on their experiences so that they can better understand what influences their interests, motivation, and learning. Second, it continues to centre student voice to allow teachers to better understand how their students are interpreting their curriculum and pedagogy.

Analyzing the Responses. In this phase, the pre-service teachers analyze the data gathered during the *Listening to Respond* phase, as well as from their observation data and reflections from the

Responding to Students phase. In this way, pre-service teachers utilize feedback from their experience as teachers and their students' experiences in the class. This analysis allows them to articulate changes they will make in their future planning and teaching, and gives them direction to the types of readings or materials they need in order to better facilitate their students' interests, motivation, and learning. Following this phase, pre-service teachers return to *Planning* and begin the process over.

The four-phase cyclical process of *Planning*, *Responding to Students*, *Listening to Respond*, and *Analyzing Responses* thus becomes student-centred inquiry *as* curriculum so that the basis of all content and pedagogical decisions arises from the reiteration of the four phases.

Listening to respond over time: what it looks like in practice

In this section we will describe a snapshot of student-centred inquiry *as* curriculum as one group of pre-service teachers from a secondary physical education methods course work with a group of 14–15 year old youth in a co-education physical education class. We will describe only the work that Oliver led with the pre-service teachers with the youth, as an example of listening and responding systematically over time. For more details on how this approach works with pre-service teachers see Oliver and Oesterreich (2013) and Oliver and Oesterreich et al. (2015).

To build the foundation with the youth, I (Kim) developed three lessons whereby pre-service teachers would work with the high school students to understand their perceptions of physical education and physical activity, understand what an emotionally and physically safe class environment entailed and collectively co-create class rules based on our understandings, and inquire into where the youth wanted to focus their learning within the context of required state physical education standards.

We began with the pre-service teachers interviewing the high school students regarding their perceptions of physical education in three broad categories: students' feelings during physical education, which included questions about what students considered fun, boring, frustrating, and embarrassing, changes students wanted to see in physical education, and peer interactions in physical education, where we asked questions such as: How do young people get along in physical education? What problems do you see? What can teachers and students do to prevent/stop these problems? Following this lesson we summarized what we had learned from the youth and came up with the major themes that influence high school students' perceptions of physical education. These students "hated running the track", "wanted more variety of activity", and "wanted more choices within the activities".

In a two-part lesson the pre-service teachers interviewed the high school students about what it meant to create a physically and emotionally safe classroom. Here we explored issues around bullying in physical education, problems that arise in physical education between students and problems that arise between students and teachers, as well as strategies for preventing problems and solving them when the arise. Utilizing what we learned, we co-created rules for a safe classroom that we all agreed to abide by for the semester. These included "be respectful – listening to whomever is talking and with equipment", "encourage each other", "try everything once", "bring a positive attitude to class", and "be safe – no bullying or ignoring people".

The final lesson was designed to inquire into students' learning interests within the required physical education state standards. Here, we worked with the high school students to help them learn what was expected learning across their high school years then to select which standards or benchmarks they thought would be most useful to learn now. This lesson served two functions: first, it allowed the students to see what was "expected" learning in physical education, second, it helped narrow our educational focus for the semester class in ways that were realistic within the structural constraints of physical education in our local high schools.

Having analyzed what we learned across the four lessons we then moved into the four-phase cyclical process of student-centred curriculum inquiry *as*. We would cycle through the process four times during the semester as a means of designing curriculum that met the needs and interests of the group of students we were working with. The first two cycles of student-centred inquiry *as* curriculum were designed to broaden the high school students' knowledge of what was possible physical education content and explore various forms of teaching. For these two cycles we taught sampler lessons, all of which were non-traditional insofar as they did not include any team sports. Part of the reason we did not include team sports is that we were working to challenge the status quo of physical education that for far too long has been dominated by team sports (Almond, 2012). In the second two cycles we designed a thematic unit to help the students explore and experience the differences between low, moderate and vigorous physical activity. In this next section we offer an example of what one of these cyclical processes looked like during the first of the sample lessons cycle.

The focus for this cycle with the youth was to broaden their understanding of physical activity, as many held limited views of what was possible. In this phase they would have an opportunity to experience six content areas and six ways of learning. Prior to *Planning*, I assigned the pre-service teachers the teaching style they would use and placed two restrictions on their choices for content: they had to try content the students had not experienced (i.e., no team sports), and they had to relate to one of the six state physical education standards. In their lesson plans they had to articulate how what they were doing related to what they learned from the high school students about their interests, motivation, and learning. Maggee and Casey selected jump bands as their content and explained under the student voice section:

> The students acknowledge the importance of fitness, but they don't like to run. Today our lesson worked with cardiovascular endurance [Standard 3] but required no running, just jumping and interacting with their peers. The students have also voiced to us that they like to talk to one another when being physically active so this lesson gave them that opportunity as well.

Rinalldo, Lacie and Jenn wrote:

> The reason that we chose to do this activity is because it is something that the students are really not exposed to. Yoga is an activity that a lot of physical educators don't know how to teach or don't take the time to teach it... The students are consistently saying that they want to have more non-traditional activities so we figured that Yoga would definitely fall into that category.

In *Responding to Students* the pre-service teachers taught four of the six mini lessons and I taught two. The content the pre-service teachers selected included yoga, jump bands, cup staking and circuit training. During these lessons, the groups that were not teaching were observing different aspects of the class. These included "peer interactions, teacher behaviours, body language of students, students' activity time, intensity of participation, grouping, and positioning in relation to teacher". We observed these aspects in relation to the students' body size differences, skill level differences and gender differences. At the completion of the six mini lessons we moved to *Listening to Respond*. We gathered in the gym and sat in circle to debrief with the high school students. During this debriefing we discussed which teaching styles motivated the high school students to want to participate and which best facilitated their learning and interests. We discussed which content areas they preferred and would like to try again.

In the *Analyzing the Responses* phase we took all of the data from the teaching and learning of mini lessons and analyzed it for overarching themes. The pre-service teachers determined that high school students enjoyed all the content because it was "new", they liked having a "variety of activities", and they liked having the "college students participate with them". Additionally the pre-service teachers identified that the high school students, when given a choice, would prefer to be in female- or male-only groups, and that students with larger bodies were often hesitant when trying new activities. We took this information and cycled back to the planning process.

The purpose of the second cycle in the student-centred inquiry *as* curriculum process was similar to the first phase in that it was designed as a means of assisting the high school students in broadening their ideas about what types of physical activities were possible. During the *Planning* phase what the pre-service teachers were most focused on was the high school students' desire for variety. What they were focused on was "giving the students as many different activities as possible". The first group selected to do a lesson on Pilates and plyometrics. They created a 45-minute routine for each section incorporating several advanced moves within Pilates and plyometrics. The second group created a lesson on adventure education. Here they had six cooperative games the students would play. The third group created a scavenger hunt lesson plan in which students needed to be able to read maps, find directions with a compass, complete fifteen physical activities, and orienteer to find information to complete the scavenger hunt. All of these elements were designed as a race between student-groups, so that the students were attempting to do all of these things as quickly as possible. The final group created a circuit lesson whereby the high school students would move from station to station. The first circuit was golf and that included three stations within the circuit. The second circuit was disk golf and this required the students moving through a nine-hole disc golf course. The final circuit was tennis, again having three separate stations within this circuit to work on different tennis skills.

During *Responding to Students*, each of the four groups of pre-service teachers taught their lesson as they had planned. Students not teaching were collecting observational data and all students were writing reflections and doing observation homework based on the data their peers collected.

After each group taught their sampler lesson, we moved into the phase of *Listening to Respond*. During the high school students' debriefing session several of the students said that "while they liked the different activities, they wished they would have had more time to play them so that they could have learned how to do them better". This was a consistent theme with the high school students.

As we moved into *Analyzing the Responses* phase, two of the strongest themes that emerged as they analyzed the data included trying to cover too much content in too little time and the current skill level of the learner. For example, as the pre-service teachers analyzed the circuit lesson where Kandy, Ryan and Jarrod tried to teach golf, disk golf, and tennis in three 15-minute circuits to students who had not learned these activities it was noted:

> It was clear from both the observation papers and from our own observations that we needed to work more on time management. Instead of having three tasks for each lesson we should have done one maybe two in the time frame we had. In the tennis lesson students did not have time to practice long enough with each swing... Kandy's could have done away with the irons station to give students more time at the putting and chipping station. *Jarrod*

Kandy noted, "The students didn't even have time to swing the golf club before we yelled, switch" and Ryan followed with, "I didn't realize so many students couldn't throw a Frisbee".

Another lesson of analysis central to the discussion was Casey and Maggee's Pilates/plyometrics lesson. Casey noted:

> I think that I assumed that the students knew the correct positioning when they actually didn't, and if I would have taken more time to explain and demonstrate they would have been better able to complete the activities and would have felt more comfortable in their environment.

Finally, in relation to the scavenger hunt, Bianca perhaps summed it up best when she reflected, "Now the scavenger hunt. Where do I begin? I think that the scavenger hunt was a flop... After looking back, I realize that I learned more from that activity than I did from anywhere else". Daniel, one of the planners of the lesson, realized during the class period, "The kids not only could not use compasses, they didn't even know the north from south and east from west".

What was important about this cycle was that the pre-service teachers and the youth learned an important lesson, one that would not have been possible had I merely told them that what they were trying wasn't going to work. The youth learned that while variety of activity was critical to their continual motivation, variety with no time to learn was not as enjoyable as they had anticipated. The pre-service teachers learned that doing activities did not mean students would learn and that they were going to have to find ways of taking what they were learning from the youth about what motivated them and couple that with what they knew about teaching for learning.

The focus for the third and fourth cycles were to provide pre-service teachers with an opportunity to develop and teach a standards-based curricular unit that addressed the high school students' interests. It was also an opportunity for the high school students to learn a particular content area in more depth. During the *Planning* phase we knew from the high school students that their need for variety influenced their willingness to engage in class. Thus, we needed to develop a curricular unit that would allow for variety of physical activity in a standards-based unit, but also allowed them enough time to learn.

Keeping the necessity for variety in the forefront, I asked the pre-service teachers what they wanted to teach. No one had any ideas because physical education has historically focused student learning on one individual activity or sport at a time (i.e., basketball, softball). Variety in activity has been characterized in the profession as a deterrent to students becoming proficient in physical activity. After prolonged silence, I proposed that they think about teaching from a conceptual framework emanating from the standards. I recommended the possibility of teaching students about low, moderate and vigorous physical activity as a means of helping them work towards Standard 3 (Participates regularly in physical activity) and Standard 4 (Achieves and maintains a health-enhancing level of physical fitness). This allowed the pre-service teachers to create a variety of activities while focusing learning around these concepts. They thought this would be a good idea and we planned who would teach what.

In the *Responding to Students* cycle we taught the students about the concept of low, moderate and vigorous activity, how to distinguish between the three, and multiple games and activities that helped them identify and experience the differences between the concepts. Teaching thematically allowed for variety of activity while still focusing on a concept across time. We worked with the students to assist them in designing their own moderate and vigorous games in order to assess whether they had a functional understanding of the concepts we were teaching. The high school student groups then each took turns teaching their games and collectively the class put together a book of moderate and vigorous physical activity games that were interesting to teens. As part of their book, in addition to a variety of student-designed moderate to vigorous games, the high school students explored the social benefits and challenges of working in groups, the various standards that they worked towards achieving, and advice from teens to teachers about what facilitates and hinders their interest, motivation, and learning in physical education.

The example provided in this section is just one instance of our approach using student-centred inquiry *as* curriculum in order to illustrate one way of listening to respond to students over time. Even though we follow the same approach each time we work with pre-service teachers and youth, how the approach looks in practice is typically different and specific to each unit and each group. This variability of outcome is an important and desirable feature of this approach to listening to respond over time, as the prior experiences, interests and needs of specific groups of youth and their pre-service teachers are unlikely to be identical year to year. We suggest this variability of what listening and responding over time looks like in practice is likely to be the case regardless of the approach taken, if the approach genuinely connects with the experiences, needs and interests of young people.

Conclusion

The focus of this chapter has been a willingness to listen and respond to girls over time, which is a fourth critical element that features in activist work with girls in physical education. We noted three themes centred in time that are consistent across the body of activist research, time on the part of the teacher to help girls find ways to communicate what they know and how they feel, time to develop the types of relationships where girls *are* willing to tell teachers or researchers what they think and how they feel, and time to figure out in collaboration with girls how to negotiate their self-identified barriers to physical education and physical activity enjoyment and engagement. We then described one systematic way of listening and responding developed by Kim in collaboration with Heather Oesterreich, which they have named "student-centred inquiry *as* curriculum". This description was followed by an example of what this approach to listening and responding looks like in practice with youth.

Learning to listen and respond to students is never without difficulties as the collection of activist research has consistently shown. Nevertheless, as Oliver and Lalik 2004 remind us, "given that the alternative to these difficulties is inaction and the maintenance of the status quo, the only real choice we have as teachers and researchers is to imagine and enact curricula and pedagogy that have the potential for a more just world" (p. 191–192). In the next and final chapter, we consider from an activist perspective this and further issues that challenge the status quo of physical education research and practice.

References

Almond, L. (2012). *Physical education in schools* (2nd ed.). London, UK: Routledge.

Brooker, R., Kirk, D., Braiuka, S. and Bransgrove, A. (2000). Implementing a game sense approach to teaching year 8 basketball. *European Physical Education Review*, 6(1), 7–26. DOI: 10.1177/1356336X000061003

Camp, E. and Oesterreich, H.A. (2010). Uncommon teaching in common sense times: A case study of a critical multicultural educator and the academic success of diverse student populations. *Multicultural Education, 17*(2), 20–26.

Cook-Sather, A. (2006). *Education is Translation.* Philadelphia, PA: University of Pennsylvania Press.

Cook-Sather, A. (2009). *Learning from student's perspectives: A sourcebook for effective teaching*. Boulder, CO: Paradigm.

Edelsky, C. (1994). Education for democracy. *Language Arts, 71*(3), 252–257.

Enright, E. and O'Sullivan, M. (2010). "Can I do it in my pyjamas?" Negotiating a physical education curriculum with teenage girls. *European Physical Education Review, 16*, 203–222. DOI: 10.1177/1356336X10382967

Enright, E. and O'Sullivan M. (2012a). Physical education "In all sorts of corners": Student activists transgressing formal physical education curricular boundaries. *Research Quarterly for Exercise and Sport 83*, 255–267. DOI: 10.1080/02701367.2012.10599856

Enright, E. and O'Sullivan, M. (2012b). Producing different knowledge and producing knowledge differently: Rethinking physical education research and practice through participatory visual methods. *Sport, Education and Society, 17*, 35–55. DOI: 10.1080/13573322.2011.607911

Evans, J. (1986) (Ed) *Physical education, sport and schooling: Studies in the sociology of physical education*. Lewes, UK: Falmer.

Evans, J., Lopez, S., Duncan, M. and Evans, M. (1987). "Some Thoughts on the Political and Pedagogical Implications of Mixed Sex Grouping in the Physical Education Curriculum" *British Educational Research Journal*, 13(1), 59–71.

Fitzgerald, H. (2005). Still feeling like a spare piece of luggage? Embodied experiences of (dis)ability in physical education and school sport. *Physical Education and Sport Pedagogy, 10*, 41–59. DOI: 10.1080/1740898042000334908

Fitzpatrick, K. (2013). *Critical pedagogy, physical education and urban schooling*. New York, NY: Peter Lang.

Flintoff, A. (1993). Gender, PE and initial teacher education, in J. Evans (Ed.), *Equality, Education and Physical education* (pp. 184–204). London, UK: Falmer.

Gee, J.P. (2000, December). *What goes without saying: From the National Reading Panel to Ownership in Literacy*. Paper presented at the annual meeting of the National Council for Teachers of English, Milwaukee, WI.

Griffin, P.S. (1984). "Girls' participation in middle school team sports unit", *Journal of Teaching in Physical Education, 4*, 30–38.

Kirk, D. (1986). Health related fitness as an innovation in the physical education curriculum, in J. Evans (Ed.) *Physical education, sport and schooling: Studies in the sociology of physical education* (pp. 167–181). Lewes, UK: Falmer.

Locke, L.F. (1974, October-November). *The ecology of the gymnasium: What the tourist never sees*. Paper presented to the SAPECW Fall Workshop Gatlinburg, TN.

Oesterreich, H.A. (2007). From "crisis" to "activist": the everyday freedom legacy of Black feminisms. *Race, Ethnicity and Education, 10*, 1–20. DOI: 10.1080/13613320601100344

Oesterreich, H.A. and Flores, S.M. (2009). Learning to C: Visual arts education as strengths based practice in juvenile correctional facilities. *Journal of Correctional Education 60*(2), 146–162.

Oliver, K.L. (1999). Adolescent girls' body-narratives: Learning to desire and create a 'fashionable' image. *Teachers College Record, 101*(2), 220–246.

Oliver, K.L. (2001). Images of the body from popular culture: Engaging adolescent girls in critical inquiry. *Sport, Education & Society* 6, 143–164. DOI: 10.1080/13573320120084245

Oliver, K.L. (2009). What feminist activist research can do for physical education teaching and research. *Historic Traditions and Future Directions of Research on Teaching and Teacher Education in Physical Education*. In L. Housner, M. Metzler, P. Schempp, and T. Templin (Eds.). Fitness Information Technology: Morganton, WV.

Oliver, K.L. and Hamzeh, M. (2010). "The boys won't let us play": 5th grade *Mestizas* publicly challenge physical activity discourse at school. *Research Quarterly for Exercise and Sport, 81*, 39–51. DOI: 10.1080/02701367.2010.10599626

Oliver, K.L., Hamzeh, M. and McCaughtry, N. (2009). "Girly girls *can* play games/*las niñas pueden jugar tambien*": Co-creating a curriculum of possibilities with 5th grade girls. *Journal of Teaching in Physical Education, 28*, 90–110.

Oliver, K.L. and Lalik, R. (2000). *Bodily knowledge: Learning about equity and justice with adolescent girls*. New York, NY: Peter Lang Publishing, Inc.

Oliver, K.L. and Lalik, R. (2004). Critical inquiry on the body in girls' physical education classes: A critical poststructural analysis. *Journal of Teaching in Physical Education* 23, 162–195.

Oliver, K.L. and Oesterreich, H.A. (2013). Student-centred inquiry as curriculum as a model for field-based teacher education. *Journal of Curriculum Studies, 45*, 394–417.

Oliver, K.L. and Oesterreich, H.A. *with* R. Aranda, J. Archuleta, C. Blazer, K. De La Cruz, D. Martinez, J. McConnell, M. Osta, L. Parks and R. Robinson. (2015). "The sweetness of struggle": Innovation in PETE through student-centred inquiry *as* curriculum in a physical education methods course. *Physical Education and Sport Pedagogy 20*(1), 97–115. DOI: 10.1080/17408989.2013.803527

Pagano, J.A. (1993). *Exiles and communities: Teaching in the patriarchal wilderness*. Albany, NY: SUNY.

Rovegno, I., Nevett, M., Brock, S. and Babiarz, M. (2001). Teaching and learning basic invasion-game tactics in 4th grade: A descriptive study for situated and constraints theoretical perspectives. *Journal of Teaching in Physical Education*, *20*, 370–388.

Schultz, K. (2003). *Listening: A Framework for teaching Across differences*. New York, NY: Teachers College Press.

Scraton, S. (1992). *Shaping up to womanhood: Gender and girls' physical education*. Buckingham, UK: Open University Press.

Shor, I. (1992). *Empowering education: Critical teaching for social change*. Chicago, IL: University of Chicago Press.

Short, K.G. and Burke, C. (1996). Examining our beliefs and practices through inquiry. *Language Arts, 73*(2), 97–104.

Sparkes, A. (1986). Strangers and structures in the process of innovation. In J. Evans (Ed.) *Physical education, sport and schooling: Studies in the sociology of physical education* (pp. 183–194). Lewes, UK: Falmer.

Tischler, A. and McCaughtry, N. (2011) PE is not for me: When boys' masculinities are threatened. *Research Quarterly for Exercise and Sport*, *82*, 37–48. DOI: 10.1080/02701367.2011.10599720

Chapter 7

Possibilities for research and physical education from an activist perspective

Introduction

Our overarching purpose in this book has been to reconsider the topic of girls, physical education and gender from an activist perspective. We argued in Chapter 2 that the "same old story" about girls and physical education has been circulating for more than thirty years, in its current form since at least the 1970s. This narrative is expressed in various ways but it typically seeks to imply that girls are somehow to blame for their apparent reluctance to fully engage in the physical education programmes they are offered. We suggested that despite attempts by feminist scholars over the years to reframe this narrative by revealing the complexity of the issue surrounding girls' engagements with physical education, the same old story continues to surface in the popular press and other media, and indeed in the work of some researchers as well.

Consistent with this purpose to reconsider the situation of girls and physical education, in the introductory chapter we made explicit some of our underlying assumptions about working in this field. As Dewey's (1938) critical reflection on the state of progressive education in the 1930s suggests, there is much misunderstanding about the nature of student-centred pedagogy and the ways in which it differs from more traditional approaches. We think the same kind of confusion and misunderstanding is evident when activist approaches to working with girls in physical education are described and explained. We have attempted to be as clear and explicit as possible about some of the key concepts that have guided this work, including the nature of activist work itself, the nature of embodied subjectivity, pragmatism and the politics of possibility, and the task for pedagogy in physical education to focus on valuing the physically active life.

In Chapters 3 to 6 we have sought to identify new ways of working with girls in physical education in terms of the common characteristics of the published activist work to date. As we noted in the introductory chapter, we faced a number of challenges in undertaking this task as to separate out four critical elements that within the work itself are intertwined and interdependent was potentially to misrepresent the nature of an activist approach. We have tried instead to work with the notion of foregrounding one element while placing the others in the background but being clear nonetheless about the interrelationships between the elements. Chapter 6 in particular, which provides an example of one way of listening to respond to young people over time, reveals the interaction and interdependency of all four critical elements.

The four critical elements we have outlined have appeared in other physical education research projects and publications, including student-centred concepts such as student perspectives and voice, and forms of critical inquiry such as critical pedagogy. Of pressing importance, and explaining our concerns about misrepresenting activist work, is that the presence of all four elements is a distinguishing feature of this approach. In other words, to practice student-centred pedagogy by itself is insufficient, as would be pedagogies of embodiment, inquiry-based education and listening to respond over time. Indeed, as we sought to demonstrate for activist work, in practice all four of these critical elements combine in complex, interdependent ways.

The extent to which the four chapters on the critical elements move us towards the construction of a pedagogical model for working with girls in physical education will be considered later in this chapter. Part of our hesitation with this proposition, which we flagged up in the introduction to the book, is that while this book builds on activist work done with girls in physical education, we are aware that similar work is now being done with boys (Luguetti, 2014; Fitzpatrick, 2013; Tischler and McCaughtry, 2011). It may be that the four critical elements have a more general application to physical education, to include work with boys. We consider this issue further momentarily but suffice to say at this time that when we began this book project we did so with the intention of working towards the development of a model for working solely with girls in physical education.

A final purpose of this book has been to set out an agenda for future research and development work in physical education, in particular work with girls. We see the book as a starting point for further conversations about possible futures for physical education, not as an end in itself. To this effect, in the rest of this concluding chapter, we want to explore some of the implications of what we have written thus far for future research in our field, in particular centred on and anchored in an activist perspective, and for the practice of physical education within schools and other pedagogical sites.

Implications for future research

We consider three issues that have implications for future research working from an activist perspective: balancing advocacy and action, the challenge of scaling up research, and the prospects for developing a pedagogical model for working with girls from an activist approach.

Activist research: balancing advocacy and action

We noted in the introduction to this book that activist research with girls rests on three assumptions. The first is that valid knowledge is produced *in* action *with* girls, and that the experiences and understandings girls bring to their physical education classes is valuable and unique. The second is that for researchers and teachers, understanding "what is" is necessary but not sufficient for working with girls in physical education as we are concerned to make a difference for the better, we must also be concerned with "what might be". The third is that acts of social transformation through pedagogy that seek to make a difference for the better must be rooted in the local context that is formed by the experiences of girls, their teachers and their communities; there is, as Dewey (1938) wrote, "no such thing as educational value in the abstract" (p. 40).

These three assumptions about activist work underwrite our critique of the "same old story", and the four critical elements for working with girls in physical education. Although action is therefore central to this approach to activist work, it is action that is purposeful, that is theoretically informed, and that has ends in mind, notwithstanding that these ends are broadly framed and emergent in each local context. Although the local context is of vital importance in activist work as its starting point, it cannot be its end point. We think we can only make progress with the situation of girls coming to value the physically active life when activist researchers, teachers and girls themselves are able to share their experiences with and learn from others in other locales and contexts.

The approach to activist research we have outlined here, underpinned by these three assumptions, by the "major theme" of valuing the physically active life and by the four critical elements, makes it unique and distinctive as a way of practicing physical education. At the same time, as we have argued from the outset in this book, this characterization of an activist approach should be viewed, following Stenhouse (1975), as a provisional specification that requires to be tested in practice. Although we have sought to convey what we know works, drawing on the literature from the past eighteen years or more of activist research with girls, we are not claiming certainty that this approach will always work or will work everywhere it is applied. We are proposing no more than this approach is worth testing, and as it is tested we fully expect it will be reflected upon, refined and refreshed. At the same time, we think some degree of fidelity is necessary if we are to build momentum for work in physical education with girls, to undermine and subvert "the same old story", to work across local contexts, and to stay focused on what might be possible for physical education with girls.

The challenge of scaling up, and a programmatic approach

Like much of the research field of physical education and sport pedagogy (Kirk and Haerens, 2014), activist research with girls has been relatively small scale, carried out by a lone researcher or perhaps a single researcher working with a critical friend, in a specific location in which considerable time is spent, and with a relatively small number of students and their teachers. These features are necessary. We have stressed throughout this book that creating programmes that meet the needs and interests of girls at the local level is a key feature of activist research. As we showed in Chapter 6, relatively lengthy periods of fieldwork are also necessary as relationships take time to build and trust is essential to the process of productively disrupting power relations within student-centred pedagogy. Because it offers no "quick fixes", researchers who have a particular passion for and commitment to this work typically undertake activist work.

Although we do not underestimate the challenges to would-be activist scholars that the corporatized Academy presents (Kirk, 2014), we believe that it is necessary to "scale-up" this programme of research if it is to have a significant influence for the better on girls' engagements in physical education. In the context of activist research with girls, scaling-up has several features. The first of these is the numbers of participants a single project can reach. As we increase the numbers of girls, we must too increase the numbers of teachers. So in order to learn how to use an activist approach, teacher professional developement will be essential. We know that traditional forms of teacher professional learning which remove the teacher from their workplace are generally ineffective (Armour and Yelling, 2004). The bulk of this professional learning thus might best be done *in situ*, with groups of teachers in their localities, led by researchers who understand the special conditions and circumstances of these localities. There are then whole programmes of professional learning that can be developed for teachers and for researchers who will work with them.

As the numbers of teachers and students increase, we have the further challenge of increasing numbers of sites or locations. As we scale-up in terms of numbers, the fidelity challenge is amplified. A second possible feature of scaling up then is the use of a pedagogical model for working with girls in physical education. At the very least, we think the four critical elements together might feature in all work that claims to be activist. The challenge here is to balance local needs and interests with fidelity to the model. We think a models-based approach could provide a sufficient level of prescription to ensure there *is* fidelity but at the same time also leave enough space for the customization of the critical elements of the model to suit local conditions. As we have proposed, activist work includes student-centred pedagogy, a pedagogy of embodiment, inquiry-based education centred in action, and a process of listening to respond to girls over time. It also includes the key characteristics of each of these elements. So for example in student-centred pedagogy, the process of authorizing students' voices guides teachers towards valuing girls' perspectives, to be open to change, and to trust girls' insights and knowledge of their own situations. Although, as part of the scaling-up process, we think these features should all be present if we are to describe work with girls as activist, we also believe that there could be considerable opportunity available to researchers and teachers and indeed to girls themselves to operationalize these features of the critical element of student-centred pedagogy in ways that suit their local conditions and circumstances.

A third feature of scaling-up is the momentum that is gained from the accumulation of studies. Again, this is an aspect of research in physical education and sport pedagogy that is underdeveloped currently, which involves taking a programmatic approach to research in specific areas of pedagogy (Kirk and Haerens, 2014). Poor citation practices may be part of the issue here, and journal editors and reviewers as well as authors have a special responsibility to raise standards of citation practice. But we also argue that much more needs to be done to build new studies on what has been learned from previously conducted and reported research. We suggest that the identification and detailed description in Chapters 3 to 6 of the four critical elements common to existing activist research provide a means of developing a line of research that is programmatic and that could explore, for example, the tensions inherent in the ways in which activist researchers work with these elements in different and divergent local contexts.

Within this process of scaling-up activist work with girls, we stress again the importance of retaining the characteristics of "small-scaleness", particularly in terms of meeting the needs and interests of girls in their local contexts, commitment of researchers, and length of time in the field. As such, we do not anticipate that this scaling-up process will adopt the methods of the public health models of intervention with large quantitative data sets. On the contrary, we suggest a qualitative case study approach, with the accumulation of cases over time, might be a more organic means of building the collective wisdom from research studies and reporting it in a form that is inherently pedagogical (Armour, 2014).

A pedagogical model, the challenge of fidelity and activist work with boys

As we noted in the introduction, we started with an idea that this book might form the basis for the development of a pedagogical model for working with girls in physical education. As we have shared our ideas with colleagues during the writing process, we have received valuable and provocative feedback, which we agree with, on the extent to which the activist approach, as we have characterized it here, may have wider application to physical education. Nonetheless, this feedback has prompted us to be clear that the evidence base for this book has come exclusively from research with girls. There has been no parallel activist research with boys until very recently and, as we noted earlier in this chapter, some of this work remains unreported in the literature as it is only just being completed in doctoral research projects. Although we have insisted that the evidence base is in work with girls, we have made no claim that this approach could not work with boys as Oliver and Oesterreich et al.'s (2015) recent work suggests. As there is little specific evidence to draw upon, we remain open on this possibility.

One attraction of developing a pedagogical model for working with girls in physical education has already been alluded to in this chapter and in Chapter 1. Pedagogical models are designed with the explicit intention of providing some critical elements that are to a large extent prescriptive. They give the model its shape and distinctiveness and are therefore "non-negotiable" as they need to be present. But at the same time, pedagogical models are designed to leave spaces for the experts in the local context of implementation (teachers and students) to interpret and apply the critical elements in ways that meet their needs and interests. Fidelity is thus balanced with the inevitable and indeed desirable transformation of innovative ideas.

We think a whole programme of research and development could be carried out to create this pedagogical model in prototype, then "test" it and further develop it through work in specific sites with teachers and students, following a specific programme of work. The making of this model would thus be a process that could take some time, depending on how many researchers, teachers and students can be recruited to this line of work. In addition to the attraction of following this route, we remain steadfast in our opinion that girls' engagements with physical education and their coming to value the physically active life ought to be a priority for *all* physical educators, researchers and education policy makers.

We do not think that following through with such a programme of research and development work necessarily precludes the further and future development of an activist approach either with boys or more generally across physical education. But the research with boys remains to be done, or where it has been done to be reported in the peer reviewed literature, and where it has been reported in the literature to be further developed beyond the one or two papers, theses and books that currently exist. We will not know whether an activist approach can be an effective means of working with boys or in more general terms across physical education as a field, until the data is in to at least an equivalent level to the data base that now exists on work with girls. But we remain open to this possibility and would encourage researchers who wish to try this approach to work with boys to do so.

Implications for future physical education

In addition to putting forth an agenda for future research involving activist approaches to physical education, there are also implications for possible futures for school physical education as a pedagogical field. As activist research gains momentum, there will be more to say on this topic. At this point in time, we want to highlight four issues for the short-term future of physical education that we think flow from our account of activist research with girls and that in our view are pressing concerns. These are the implications of a pragmatic approach, of valuing the physically active life as a guiding principle, of the politics of student-centred pedagogy, and the need for teachers as creative, empathetic and critical individuals.

A pragmatic approach: what is best for these *girls* now?

Drawing on Dewey and post-Deweyan pragmatism, we posed three questions in the introduction to this book in relation to the politics of possibility: Can we make the situation for *these* girls better than it is currently? What would be better? *How* might we go about this task? We think it is by posing these questions or questions like them that we are most likely, in the short term, to be able to work with girls to meet their needs and interests in physical education, rather than relying on the mandated imposition of national curricula or standards alone. Despite the undoubted attraction of the possibilities of such curricular initiatives for equal opportunities and uniform provision, we think they need to be written in such a way as to empower teachers and their students to take actions that are congruent with and organic within their local contexts. Currently, even the most sophisticated of these initiatives have the potential to constrain what is possible in local contexts as they rest on the same assumptions of traditional education, that there is a recognized and settled "cultural heritage" that is common to the whole population and that deserves to be celebrated and reproduced in and through schools (Kirk, 2010). We will say a little more about the counterpoint to this traditionalist assumption momentarily.

The challenges confronting girls and their engagement (or non-engagement) with physical education and thus with the physical culture of society at large are urgent and pressing. The consequences of this non-engagement are damaging for their prospects in life. Given what is at stake, we think that a pragmatic approach, which focuses on the local context as its starting point, trumps other approaches that inevitably rest on a notion of "educational value in the abstract". As we have shown through the chapters of this book, girls and their experiences, interests and knowledge form the basis of an activist approach. We know from a critical mass of research in this field that a root cause of girls' disengagements with physical education are that many prescriptions that derive from the assumed universal cultural heritage of society mean little or nothing to them. Within the narrative of "the same old story", it is girls who are to blame for this lack of meaningfulness. Within an activist approach guided by these pragmatic questions, we begin to see that it is girls' experiences and knowledge that shape what physical education might be and how they might benefit from it.

Valuing the physically active life: a guiding principle

We suggest in Chapter 5 one of the radical implications of inquiry-based education centred *in* action is that the organizing centre for physical education inevitably shifts from the sports and games that characterize traditional programmes to programmes that are shaped by the needs and interests of girls in specific local contexts. One possible reaction to this development that we flag in Chapter 5 could be the concern that "anything goes", that physical education loses its distinctive character and thus its unique contribution to the school curriculum. There is a danger here, perhaps, for physical education's potential demise if physical education policy-makers do not, as is common in some countries such as the UK, specify uniform content or standards based on a notion of "universal cultural heritage".

A focus on valuing the physically active life acts as a counterweight to this reaction and as a guiding principle of the focus and substance of physical education within an activist approach. There are at least three features of this notion of valuing the physically active life that are important to consider in this regard. The first is that it is likely to have universal buy-in from policy-makers, educational professionals and the lay public. This is because it is now widely recognized that regular physical activity is an essential component of a healthy lifestyle. The notion of valuing the physically active life also works at a number of levels. For universal buy-in among the population at large, it seems simple and self-evident. But a second feature of this notion, and where it works at an altogether more complex level, is the focus on valuing. As we noted in the introduction to this book, valuing encompasses what people think and do, but it also goes beyond knowledge and behaviour to what people feel and what they believe. Educating young people to *value* is far from simple and self-evident, but it *is* more likely to have an enduring and sustainable effect on young people's dispositions to habitually and routinely make time to be active, even in the face of attractive alternatives.

A third feature is the necessity of participation in physical activity. The requirement for girls to be physically active in the process of coming to value the physically active life acts as a counter-point to concerns that the pragmatic character of an activist approach might jeopardize physical education's place in the curriculum. No other pedagogical field in schools is concerned with organized and purposeful physical activity and it seems to us unlikely that teachers of other school subjects would ever seek out this responsibility. Moreover, the notion of physical activity itself is broad and inclusive enough to permit a wide range of possible forms of physical education. Seidentop (1996) argued that valuing involves participation in physical activity, but also involves a willingness to participate in ways that are literate and critical. Literacy, concerned with knowledgeable and activist participation, and criticality, concerned with understanding and acting to eliminate structural inequalities that constrain participation, provide further guidance to physical educators for how valuing the physically active life can work as a guiding principle for activist researchers and teachers.

The politics of student-centred pedagogy

The implications for conventional forms of physical education of an activist approach guided by pragmatic questions may seem radical enough in themselves. The three pragmatic questions in turn raise further fundamental questions about the nature of the physical cultures of society, *whose* selections of physical cultures are drawn down from the universe of physical cultural possibilities, and what the accepted and socially approved forms of engagement with the "products" (such as physical education curricula), of physical cultures are. Student-centred pedagogy, as we have outlined it in Chapter 3, is of central importance to an activist approach as it forms a basis on which activist researchers and teachers can work with girls in physical education. As authorizing student voice requires the productive disruption of power relations, it challenges schools in a most fundamental way, in particular their hierarchies of authority and power. Posing these pragmatic questions is therefore to highlight the politics of student-centred pedagogy and to expose the power relations that maintain conventional forms of schooling.

Working with an activist approach within a single pedagogical field such as physical education may present a big enough challenge. But what might the implications be for the whole school curriculum? Is it possible to take such an approach in one curriculum area yet expect the power relations of the school to remain intact in all other areas? We think this is unlikely because girls themselves immediately recognize the differences in the ways they are recognized, treated and valued within the same institution. Giving girls a voice in one subject area could create a demand for similar authorizing in others.

Although our concern here is specifically working with girls in physical education, we think there are quite profound implications of an activist approach for other pedagogical fields in the school and, indeed, for the structure and operation of the school itself. In the first place, can physical education teachers work with teachers in other fields to develop an activist approach across the curriculum? Not only does this question raise further issues of new skills physical educators may need to develop, including collaborative work and advocacy skills, but it also begs further questions about the subject-specific organization of the curriculum particularly in secondary schools. Second, student-centred pedagogy within an activist approach highlights shortcomings of the traditional notion of the school, which have been widely criticized since at least the 1960s with calls for alternative forms of schooling (Holt, 1967) and to de-school society (Illich, 1971) through to the present time with explorations of new institutional designs (Lawson, 2013). We anticipate that these challenges will need to be faced as we begin to scale-up activist work in physical education. The possibilities for the success of this process will, in our view, hang in the more immediate short term on the quality of physical education teachers who are willing to become involved in an activist programme of work.

Teachers as creative, empathetic and critical individuals

The politics of student-centred pedagogy exposes a range of challenges implicit in an activist approach to working with girls. It may be challenging enough to contemplate how such work can proceed in a single pedagogical field, never mind across the entire curriculum. Although we think physical educators need to be aware of the bigger challenges posed by cross-curricular collaboration and the need for new organizational forms of schooling, we do not believe it is part of our core business at this stage in the development of activist work to take these challenges on in the short term, nor by ourselves. Such work will require careful consideration, the formation of collaborative partnerships across schools, universities and communities, and new skills in evidence-based advocacy and policy-development. In the shorter term and pragmatically, we think that among our immediate priorities is the need to identify the kinds of teachers who can take forward an activist approach with girls as we seek to scale up this programme of work.

Dewey (1938) noted a widespread assumption that in progressive forms of education where the learners' experiences are of central concern, the teacher's experience is unimportant. On the contrary, he argued:

> On the one side, it is his (sic: the male adult's) business to be on the alert to see what attitudes and habitual tendencies are being created. In this direction he must, if he is an educator, be able to judge what attitudes are actually conducive to continued growth and what are detrimental. He must, in addition, have that sympathetic understanding of individuals as individuals which gives him an idea of what is actually going on in the minds of those who are learning. It is, among other things, the need for these abilities on the part of the parent and

> teacher which makes a system of education based upon living experience a more difficult affair to conduct successfully than it is to follow the patterns of traditional education (pp. 38–39).

In short, Dewey's claim was that far from being marginal or irrelevant, teachers of progressive forms of education are of central importance to its successful conduct. In the statement just quoted, Dewey signals clearly the kinds of skills and dispositions such a teacher needs to possess. These include the ability to observe learners closely, and to judge how experience may be developed to stimulate further development and growth. Teachers also need sympathetic and empathetic understanding of young people, to be able in a sense to stand in their shoes, and to see the world from the learner's point of view.

Although we make no claim that this description of the teacher of progressive forms of education is new (Dewey was writing in the 1930s), we wonder to what extent such teachers are commonplace and widespread in physical education. We think the advocacies for critical pedagogy in physical education teacher education since the 1980s may have had *some* influence in terms of alerting new generations of physical educators to the social injustices of some aspects of physical cultural practices and the need to address these. But we are less sure that advocacy for student-centred physical educators has been heard.

This should come as no surprise to us as there is widespread acknowledgement in the physical education teacher education literature that teachers in this field have tended to be teachers first of the subject, then of young people. Physical educators have a reputation, perhaps less deserved now than in the past, of being authoritarian and directive. There *are* creative, empathetic and socially-critical physical education teachers in our field, though the extent to which they are able to practice aspects of activist work with young people may be circumscribed by strongly held professional and public perceptions of the nature of physical education (Ives and Kirk, 2013).

We think an immediate priority is to identify and nurture teachers who have the qualities of judgment, the skills of observation, the dispositions of empathy, and who have an interest in and commitment to activist work in physical education. The professional development of such teachers working in collaboration with like-minded activist researchers is, we think, the best and most immediate strategy to take forward the research agenda outlined earlier in this chapter and throughout this book and to influence the ways in which physical education is conceptualized and practiced in schools. We need teachers and researchers who not only understand "what is" the current situation of working with girls in physical education, but who also, in Freire's terms, have the *courage to love*, and are thus committed to exploring *and* enacting with girls "what might be".

References

Armour, K.M. (2014, ed) *Pedagogical cases in physical education and youth sport*. London, UK: Routledge.

Armour, K.M. and Yelling, M.R. (2004) Continuing professional development for experienced physical education teachers: towards effective provision. *Sport, Education and Society*, 9, 95–114. DOI: 10.1080/1357332042000175836

Dewey, J. (1938) *Education and experience*. New York, NY: Macmillan.

Fitzpatrick, K. (2013). *Critical pedagogy, physical education and urban schooling*. New York, NY: Peter Lang.

Holt, J. (1967). *How Children Learn*. New York, NY: Pitman Publishing Corporation.

Illich, I. (1971). *Deschooling Society*. New York, NY: Harper and Row.

Ives, H. and Kirk, D. (2013). What are the public perceptions of physical education? In S. Capel and M. Whitehead (Eds.), *Debates in Physical Education* (pp. 188–202). London, UK: Routledge.

Kirk, D. (2010). *Physical education futures*. London, UK: Routledge.

Kirk, D. (2014) Making a career in PESP in the corporatized university: reflections on hegemony, resistance, collegiality and scholarship. *Sport, Education and Society* 19(3), 320–332.

Kirk, D. and Haerens, L. (2014). New research programmes in physical education and sport pedagogy. *Sport, Education and Society*, *19*, 899–911. DOI: 10.1080/13573322.2013.874996

Lawson, H.A. (2013). Appreciating complexity, endemic tensions and selectivity in proposals for program improvement and new institutional designs. *Sport, Education and Society*, *18*, 121–129. DOI: 10.1080/13573322.2012.685708

Luguetti, C.N. (2014). *Moving from what is to what might be: developing a prototype pedagogical model of sport addressed to boys from socially vulnerable backgrounds in Brazil* (Unpublished doctoral dissertation). University of Sao Paulo, Butantã, Brazil.

Oliver, K.L. and Oesterreich, H.A. *with* R. Aranda, J. Archuleta, C. Blazer, K. De La Cruz, D. Martinez, J. McConnell, M. Osta, L. Parks and R.

Robinson. (2015). "The sweetness of struggle": Innovation in PETE through student-centred inquiry *as* curriculum in a physical education methods course. *Physical Education and Sport Pedagogy 20*(1), 97–115. DOI: 10.1080/17408989.2013.803527

Siedentop, D. (1996). Valuing the physically active life: Contemporary and future directions. *Quest,* 48, 266–274. DOI: 10.1080/00336297.1996.10484196

Stenhouse, L. (1975). *An introduction to curriculum research and development.* London, UK: Heinemann.

Tischler, A. and McCaughtry, N. (2011) PE is not for me: When boys' masculinities are threatened. *Research Quarterly for Exercise and Sport, 82*, 37–48. DOI: 10.1080/02701367.2011.10599720

Index

Note: Page numbers followed by "f" refer to figures.